SELF-DETERMINATION
IN THE
NEW WORLD ORDER

SELF-DETERMINATION IN THE NEW WORLD ORDER

Morton H. Halperin and David J. Scheffer
with Patricia L. Small

Carnegie Endowment for International Peace
Washington, D.C.

Library of Congress Cataloging-in-Publication Data

Halperin, Morton H.
    Self-determination in the new world order / Morton H. Halperin and
David J. Scheffer with Patricia L. Small.
        p.   cm.
    Includes bibliographical references and index.
    ISBN 0-87003-018-3 : $21.95. — ISBN 0-87003-019-1 (pbk.) : $8.95
    1. Self-determination, National.   2. United States—Foreign
relations—1989–   I. Scheffer, David.   II. Small, Patricia L.
(Patricia Louise), 1969–   .   III. Title.
JX4054.H33   1992
327.73—dc20   92-23015
                                                                    CIP

Printed on Recycled Paper

To Carol Pitchersky

Walter and Barbara Scheffer

and Chester and Evelyn Small

CONTENTS

FOREWORD

by Lloyd N. Cutler[1]

"Self-determination" is one of those unexceptionable goals that can be neither defined nor opposed. It can mean the right of people to choose their own form of government within existing borders, for example by overturning a dictatorship or achieving independence from a colonial power. It can mean the right of an ethnic, linguistic, or religious group to redefine existing national borders in order to achieve separate national sovereignty. It can mean the right of a political unit within a federal system, such as Canada, Czechoslovakia, the former Soviet Union, or the former Yugoslavia, to secede from the federation and become an independent sovereign state. Or it can merely mean the right of an ethnic, linguistic, or religious group within an existing sovereign state to a greater degree of autonomy and linguistic or religious identity, but not to a sovereign state of its own.

Self-determination is also in tension with other unexceptionable concepts, such as the inviolability of national borders and non-interference in the internal affairs of other states. Indeed, before the crisis in Yugoslavia in 1991 and 1992, the policy of the United Nations, colonial wars aside, was to abstain from intervening in civil wars of self-determination such as those in Nigeria in the late 1960s and in Pakistan in 1971.

But as the authors of this valuable study point out, the international community's ideas about self-determination are changing. Under the banner of self-determination, there are active movements in more than sixty countries—one third of the total roster of nations—to achieve full sovereignty or some lesser degree of "minority" rights. A number of these movements have developed into ongoing civil wars. International rules about non-intervention

---

[1]*Counsel, Wilmer, Cutler & Pickering; former Counsel to President Jimmy Carter; Member, U.S. Group, Permanent Court of Arbitration, The Hague.*

in other nations' civil wars are giving way to the idea that civil wars can threaten world peace and that international institutions should move to contain such threats by mediation and, if need be, more coercive measures. Moreover, the nineteenth century idea that a federal state had the right to repress any attempted secession by force—the right over which we fought our bloody Civil War—is also becoming outmoded. Many modern federations have constitutions that expressly permit voluntary secession, and in those where the constitution is silent on the matter—as in Canada and Czechoslovakia—no one speaks of using force to confront the existing secessionist movements.

Indeed, the use of force to put down a self-determination movement is almost guaranteed to earn worldwide disapproval today. Self-determination, although a collective rather than an individual claim, is rapidly moving into the category of internationally recognized human rights, upon which no state can infringe without objection—and sometimes intervention—by the international community.

The Carnegie study is the first of its kind. It analyzes the new spate of self-determination movements and the international community's efforts to deal with them. It recognizes the practical difficulties of resolving some of these claims, such as centuries-old blood feuds and migration checkerboards that make ethnically pure borders impossible. The authors also recognize the political difficulties of achieving consensus among permanent and other U.N. Security Council members with self-determination problems of their own (for example, the United Kingdom with Scotland, France with Corsica, and China with Tibet). Nevertheless, they suggest bold new policies for the United States and the international community, aimed not only at dealing with threats to peace after they arise, but also at mediating and resolving self-determination claims before they become threats to peace. This study is timely, informative, provocative, and a significant contribution to the debate over one of the most complex challenges of our time.

ACKNOWLEDGMENTS

This book has been prepared as part of the Project on Self-Determination of the Carnegie Endowment for International Peace. We want to thank the Endowment for its financial and administrative support in this endeavor. A study group was formed at the Endowment in November 1991 to examine various developments in self-determination. Members of the study group who are in a position to have their names listed are identified on pages 163 and 164. The group met four times and engaged in lengthy discussions on a wide range of issues relating to self-determination. We also received comments on early drafts of the book from Louis B. Sohn, Leon Sigal, Lloyd N. Cutler, Jenonne Walker, Stanley J. Heginbotham, Edwin M. Smith, Michael W. Doyle, Frank Koszorus, Pauline Baker, James Clad, Paul Goble, Jane E. Stromseth, Larry Fabian, and Morton I. Abramowitz. We deeply thank all of these individuals for their contributions to this study.

We could not have undertaken or completed this book without the talented assistance of our co-author, Patricia L. Small. She brought to the research and drafting a tireless commitment and the rare talent to excel professionally within a year of graduating from college in a field that challenges seasoned experts. She is to be credited for researching the global survey on self-determination movements that appears in the appendix, a feat that we strongly recommend the U.S. government now undertake on an annual basis (see page 98).

We also received expert help from Rosemarie Philips, our copy editor, and Rhonda Hudanish, Connie Mitchell, and Glenn Pierce of The Magazine Group, which designed the book.

The support staff at the Endowment provided invaluable assistance in the production of the book. They include Jennifer Little (librarian), Lynn Meininger, Chris Henley, Toula Papanicolas, Anne K. Svoboda, and intern

Susan Rezabek. Robin Ayers, an Endowment intern, skillfully maintained our database. Marinn Carlson and Daniel Prieto assisted with research. We are also grateful to the president and secretary of the Endowment for their commitment to this project. Michael V. O'Hare, the Endowment's chief administrator, was extremely helpful in arranging the production of the book.

The Endowment's sponsorship of this project reflects its belief in the importance of the subject. The treatment of the subject and the views expressed, however, are entirely the responsibility of the authors.

Finally, we want to express our deep appreciation to our wives, whose support and patience inspired our work.

Morton H. Halperin
David J. Scheffer
Washington, D.C.
August 1992

INTRODUCTION

The vision of a "new world order" since 1990 has been a world with one superpower—the United States—in which the rule of law supplants the rule of the jungle, disputes are settled peacefully, aggression is firmly met by collective resistance, and all people are justly treated.[1] But a peaceful, stable, and just new world order has not yet come to pass. In June 1991, Yugoslavia descended into a civil conflict that left nearly 20,000 dead and more than one million homeless within a year. Three of the successor states of the Soviet Union—Georgia, Tajikistan, and Azerbaijan—have experienced power struggles over control of their governments involving varying degrees of violence. Ethnic disputes are underway or loom in the new states of Azerbaijan, Georgia, Moldova, Russia, and Ukraine. In Somalia, 30,000 died and up to 2.5 million were forced to flee their homes between January 1991 and July 1992, in the face of civil war, anarchy, and mass starvation.

No one can argue that these events were desirable. From a humanitarian perspective, the level of suffering is staggering. The vision of a peaceful new world order did not anticipate how frequently groups in the midst of these struggles would invoke the principle of "self-determination." Although the term's precise meaning is a matter of controversy, at its simplest the principle of self-determination accords people a right to govern their own affairs. Throughout the Cold War, this principle provided colonial peoples with the foundation for their claims to freedom from foreign rule. Now, in the

---

[1] Statements of President George Bush, September 11, 1990, January 29, 1991, and April 13, 1991. Reprinted in *Public Papers of the Presidents of the United States: George Bush, 1990*, Book II (Washington, D.C.: U.S. Government Printing Office, 1991), p. 1219; *Public Papers of the Presidents of the United States: George Bush, 1991*, Book I (Washington, D.C.: U.S. Government Printing Office, 1992), pp. 79 and 366.

post–Cold War world, groups within states are staking claims to independence, greater autonomy, or the overthrow of an existing government, all in the name of self-determination.

What lessons are to be drawn, for example, from the violent breakup of Yugoslavia? Some observers have argued that the United States has neither the power nor the interests to justify intervention in such conflicts. Rather, the United States should remain aloof and send humanitarian aid only when the violence has ended. For these observers, the U.S. government risked exacerbating and being drawn into the conflict by giving hope of support to both sides.

Others, including at least some officials in the U.S. government, argued that the international community, by entertaining the possibility of recognizing Yugoslavia's seceding states and by ultimately doing so, brought leaders of Croatia and Bosnia-Herzegovina to believe that they could lead their republics out of Yugoslavia with the military support of at least a few major powers. Those leaders learned quickly, however, that the world community would essentially acquiesce in a central government's aggressive use of force to slaughter ethnic rivals and seize sovereign land with impunity. The lesson for the future was that the United States should make clear to a secessionist movement that it will get no support from the United States, while the existing government can expect no or minimal interference in its attempt to preserve the status quo. A clear policy of resistance to secession would impress upon a self-determination movement that it must seek accommodation of its wishes within existing borders.

There is a third possibility. By standing back and advocating Yugoslav unity during the months leading up to the crisis, the international community led Belgrade to believe that it had a free hand to do whatever was necessary to keep Yugoslavia together or, at a minimum, create a Greater Serbia. Instead, the United States and the international community should have adopted a more activist approach earlier, pressing the Yugoslav government to accommodate the aspirations of self-determination movements within its borders. Remaining aloof or blindly siding with an existing government can lead to, rather than prevent, conflict. In many situations, an activist approach will mean pressing for some form of local autonomy, perhaps in a federated system; in other cases, it might well mean supporting the creation of a new independent state.

Many, perhaps most, Americans still support the first or second perspective. However, we believe that the U.S. government should take the lead in coordinating a more activist international response to self-determination crises. We are not unaware of the obstacles to such an approach. Few Americans are eager for responsibilities abroad. Many nations, whose support would be necessary, are equally skeptical. Aside from threats to international peace and security, the number of which are expanding,[2] international law provides little support for unilateral intervention in the internal affairs of states confronting self-determination movements and is only beginning to consider what might justify multilateral intervention.

Having conceded all of this, we nonetheless argue that American interests and ideals compel a more active role. An American president and the U.S. government can with determined leadership move the American people and other nations to accept the need for early measures to manage the resolution of self-determination claims. International law—as it always has done—will respond and adjust to the behavior of nations and the actions of multilateral institutions.

Some readers doubtless will view our proposals as unrealistic—as yet another manifestation of Wilsonian idealism, out of touch with domestic and international realities. In fact, we are far removed from Wilsonian idealism. The whole purpose of this book is to confront realities rather than to ignore them.

By August 1992 governments were facing demands from their citizens and politicians to do more in Bosnia-Herzegovina and Somalia in the face of growing evidence of human catastrophe. We believe that a failure to respond more quickly, directly, and comprehensively to self-determination claims in the future will cause more such needless tragedy and suffering around the globe, ultimately with profound consequences for U.S. interests and American ideals.

Each reader will have to assess which of the three approaches to self-determination—aloofness, support for central governments, early action to promote resolution—is in the national interest. If one agrees that the steps proposed in this book are desirable, one can still conclude that there is no likelihood of their being adopted by the U.S. government or of gaining the necessary support from other nations. Perhaps that will be the outcome no

---

[2]See "Security Council Summit Declaration: 'New Risks for Stability and Security,'" *New York Times*, February 1, 1992, p. 4 ("The non-military sources of instability in the economic, social, humanitarian and ecological fields have become threats to peace and security.").

matter what is done. However, those who believe that our interests lie elsewhere should not remain silent for fear of being accused of being unrealistic or idealistic.

Self-Determination Movements after the Cold War

While the Cold War created an artificial stability that muzzled much
ethnic and separatist activism, the struggles and the violence are not new.
China's suppression of an uprising in Tibet in 1959 left more than one million people dead. Five hundred thousand people died in Ethiopia's thirty-
year struggle to hold onto its northern province of Eritrea. Some of Western Europe's separatist struggles—in the Basque regions of France and Spain
and in Northern Ireland—are decades old.

Two aspects of self-determination disputes are new, however, in the
post–Cold War world. First, the breakup of the Soviet Union dwarfed any
self-determination struggle during the Cold War. That event, and the
readiness of the international community to accept the emergence of new
states, is likely to embolden groups within other states to stake claims to
self-determination.

Second, with the end of the Cold War, the world community has an
opportunity to work together to better manage self-determination claims.
Much depends on whether the United States, as the world's lone superpower,
can use its leadership and leverage to help prevent self-determination disputes from erupting into crises of the magnitude of that in Yugoslavia.

The United States and the rest of the world community, however, remain
hobbled by the perspectives of the Cold War. Events in the Soviet Union
and Yugoslavia in 1991 and 1992 challenged prevailing notions about the
stability of national borders. Still, the American people and their leaders initially were surprised by the dismantlement of these multiethnic states and the
much-desired collapse of the totalitarian regimes that had long sustained them.
There was little popular dissent over U.S. support for efforts to preserve either state, even when it was clear that movements toward breakup were too
strong to resist. Other countries shared this perspective, reflecting the dominant view that existing states had the right and the duty to resist secessionist
efforts. International law had long embodied this view, limiting the legal right
of self-determination to colonial peoples struggling for independence.

Most observers thought that the future would bring the further integration of existing states, such as European union and closer cooperation among

states to solve global problems such as environmental pollution. Secessionist movements were viewed in large part as "tribal" vestiges of a bygone era. A few took the opposite and equally naive view that striving for self-determination embodied all that was noble and good. They believed that the Wilsonian vision of self-determination would at last be realized around the globe with a vast collection of states, each occupied by a people who had exercised the right of self-determination, living in peace with one another.

The political upheavals of the post–Cold War world are occurring in a wide spectrum of societies and regions. The disintegration of Yugoslavia added four new countries to the map and triggered terrible conflicts. The collapse of the Soviet Union brought 15 new states onto the world stage. Separatism among Russia's autonomous republics threatens that state's integrity. Ethnic turmoil within Nagorno-Karabakh promises continued conflict between Armenia and Azerbaijan. The fate of Kashmir—suspended for almost 50 years—may finally be determined, perhaps violently. As victims of numerous atrocities by the government of Saddam Hussein, the Kurds and the Shia of Iraq are struggling to protect their very existence—either within Iraq (through autonomy or the transformation of the Baghdad regime into a democratic government) or by seceding. The people of Haiti suffered another military dictatorship shortly after adopting democratic government. China maintains its hold on Tibet. With its main opposition party advocating formal independence from mainland China, Taiwan may yet experience internal upheaval or communist aggression as its final status is determined. The independence movement within Scotland persists. The future of the Palestinian people remains uncertain as negotiators struggle with novel theories of autonomy, citizenship, territorial jigsaws, and independent statehood. Throughout Africa, the pressures of self-determination are increasing and threatening the stability of post-colonial borders.[3]

At the same time, the utopian view of such movements and of the ease with which the transition to a new world order would occur has also been shattered. The carnage in, and refugee flows from, Bosnia-Herzegovina remove any doubt that the drive for self-determination is fraught with danger for the people involved and serious consequences for the rest of the world. The real issue is whether the United States and the world community can simply stand by and watch violent struggles unfold in country after country.

---

[3]See the Appendix for a survey of self-determination movements around the world.

The process may be messier and in some cases, if the world remains aloof, even more violent than in Yugoslavia. Most situations giving rise to claims of self-determination will not involve the collapse of central authority. Rather, an existing government will face the prospect that some of its territory seeks to break away to form an independent state or to acquire a greater degree of political or cultural autonomy. Many self-determination movements have an even broader goal—to replace the existing central government with one that is more representative and more humane. In some cases, the challenge may be limited to achieving adequate protection of minority rights within a state dominated by another ethnic group.

The Need for U.S. Leadership

How the United States responds to each of these challenges to the status quo will say much about the character and influence of U.S. foreign policy following the Cold War. As the sole remaining superpower and the world's leading democracy, the United States plays a critical role both in maintaining international peace and security among states and in upholding the principles and values that should underpin self-determination movements. During the Cold War, U.S. policy toward movements seeking to break off from an existing state or to create a new political arrangement were governed by the imperative of the superpower struggle; such demands were resisted for the sake of stability unless they were seen as part of the effort to contain the Soviet Union. With that imperative removed, a new policy is both necessary and desirable.

The United States has not yet developed a comprehensive set of principles and standards for responding to self-determination movements. The consequence has been that the United States lurches from one self-determination crisis to the next—pulling back one day, charging ahead the next, and too often abdicating responsibility or leadership in managing an international response.

If the world community is to develop a common approach to deal with self-determination crises, the United States must take the lead. No other nation or group of nations has the global interests or the political will to lead. The United States should not act alone, but rather should work with other governments through the United Nations and appropriate regional organizations. The interests of the United States—to prevent war, to avoid human suffering, to promote the right of all individuals to pursue their destiny in peace as they choose—are interests shared by much of the world community and increasingly embodied in international and regional agreements. Even with determined leadership by the U.S. government, gaining the necessary support at home and abroad will take years and entail very difficult policy choices. In some situations this may mean that no action is possible or that the U.S. government may determine that its interests are so directly affected that it must act alone.

Since we write as Americans, we present a new approach to handling self-determination movements from an American perspective. Although we draw on specific cases to illustrate our points, we do not offer concrete solutions for any particular case or even a road map for dealing with a specific crisis. We argue that the United States and the international community should adopt a more systematic approach to the challenges posed by self-determination movements. The application of the general approach we suggest to specific challenges will require creative policy that takes into account the particulars of each situation.

We approach this task with a few key assumptions:

- self-determination claims can reflect genuine drives and legitimate aspirations that must not be ignored;
- in most cases, such aspirations can and should be fulfilled within the borders of existing states by such means as respect for individual rights as well as the rights of minority groups seeking to promote their separate identity;
- in some cases, new states will need to be created, despite the danger of such transitions for the people involved and for the world; and
- the United States and the world community have interests that should lead to early involvement in such self-determination disputes, first to urge internal changes that may dampen pressures for secession and, if that fails, to seek a peaceful process of change towards secession.

In arguing that the United States in particular should concern itself with such struggles long before refugees stream across international borders, we recognize that this cuts against the grain of the current focus on domestic priorities; the American "mood" still swings between isolationism and interventionism. We also are aware that such efforts will be viewed with suspicion by many other nations. Nonetheless, a strong case can be made for American leadership in the creation of a new world order.[4]

---

[4]See Carnegie Endowment National Commission on America and the New World, *Changing Our Ways* (Washington, D.C.: Carnegie Endowment for International Peace, 1992).

American ideals and self-interest merge when the United States supports the spread of democracy around the globe—or what we prefer to call "limited" constitutional democracy, meaning rule by a government that has been legitimized by free elections. New governments must respect the rights of their citizens to dissent from public policies and to be free of arbitrary arrest, detention, and torture. They must respect the distinctive characteristics of the minority groups within their borders. Regimes governed by a rule of law are less likely to resort to violence across their borders and more likely to pursue economic policies that contribute to prosperity in the United States.

To gain the support of the American people, U.S. policies on self-determination should focus on promoting the creation of constitutional democracies. Such governments embody the ideals of the American people and stand a better chance of contributing to the peaceful and prosperous world desired by Americans. Dealing creatively with the dangers and opportunities of self-determination movements is one key to moving toward a world in which there are more such constitutional democracies. The relationship between democracy and self-determination is not, however, straightforward.

It was precisely the spread of democracy in the Soviet Union and portions of Yugoslavia that doomed those multiethnic states. Once people were free to express their political aspirations without fear of brutal suppression, those who sought the creation of independent states were able to seek support for their views. Demands for independence grew before efforts could be made to persuade people that their desires could be fulfilled within a newly-constructed federal state with guarantees of genuine autonomy and democracy.

There may be other situations in which the desire for independence is so strong and so widely held that granting democratic rights will only accelerate the breakup of a state. However, in most situations the key to preserving a state is to grant full democracy to all of its people, including those who see themselves as part of a minority. Only a state that guarantees its citizens full political, civil, and human rights can persuade those citizens to seek an accommodation of their demands within the existing state.

Thus, if the United States decides that a self-determination claim is justified, Washington should first urge the ruling government to make the reforms necessary to create a constitutional democracy that accommodates the claim. Only if that effort fails should the United States take the lead or join with other governments in supporting a self-determination movement seeking separate statehood.

A more timely and sophisticated U.S. treatment of self-determination needs to be understood by Americans as a key component of the nation's support for democracy abroad. Governments that remain repressive out of fear of unleashing self-determination movements must be persuaded that such efforts are ultimately self-defeating. A group claiming a right to self-determination must come to understand that if it seeks the assistance of the United States and the world community, it first should seek an accommodation of its interests within existing state borders. If that effort fails and the group advocates secession, it must commit to creating and maintaining a constitutional democracy, including the protection of individual and minority rights, if it is to gain support for the creation of a new state.

The Need for a Multilateral Response

A more active self-determination policy cannot be premised, however, on a unilateral approach. While the United States should not forfeit its right to use military force unilaterally in accordance with international law when significant U.S. interests are directly threatened, Americans will not countenance U.S. intervention in more ambiguous situations unless other states share the burden in terms of blood as well as treasure.

The importance of responding collectively rather than unilaterally in self-determination disputes is an imperative not only of domestic politics but also of international politics. Many other governments and observers view "self-determination" as only the latest pretext for self-interested intervention by the United States. The belief persists that U.S. imperialism in part explains U.S. actions during the Cold War and that U.S. imperial interests are being reasserted even after the collapse of the other superpower.

The United States thus will need to work with other governments to inform and to support its own judgment about the character and future prospects of various self-determination movements. At the same time, the United States should avoid coercive forms of intervention—economic embargoes, blockades, or military actions—except when sanctioned by the U.N. Security Council or an appropriate regional body.

In collaborating with other governments on responses to self-determination disputes, the United States will need to recognize that many states approach this issue faced with their own internal problems. A state with an active or latent self-determination movement, particularly one that has claimed or could claim the right to secede, will be cautious about supporting a policy that contemplates intervention in what it views as the internal affairs of a state. Each of the other four permanent members of the U.N. Security Council struggles with its own internal self-determination movements. The United States will need to act as often as possible on the basis of universal principles enunciated in advance and applied uniformly in order to build support among other governments in specific situations.

The adoption of a new approach for dealing with self-determination movements will never be a substitute for wisdom and statesmanship in dealing with specific crises. But it is because we believe that a conceptual framework moving beyond Cold War perspectives is a prerequisite for any successful policy that we have written this book.

Chapter One

SELF-DETERMINATION CLAIMS
DURING THE COLD WAR

D uring the Cold War, the United States and the world community exhibited great skepticism toward self-determination claims, except for those that were viewed as demands for independence from colonial rule.

The U.S. Response

I n general, the United States resisted non-colonial self-determination claims during the Cold War on the basis of five principles. The first two principles followed from the Cold War confrontation with the Soviet Union. Two other principles related specifically to self-determination and the stability of states. A final principle reflected American ambivalence about overseas commitments.

Determine support for a self-determination movement by assessing its potential impact on the worldwide struggle with the Soviet Union. The United States opposed so-called "separatist" movements in allied countries; many independence movements were viewed as being communist-inspired and hence contrary to U.S. interests. Washington supported the efforts of Marshal Josip Broz Tito to hold together a federal Yugoslavia, because a unified Yugoslavia was seen as an effective counterweight to Soviet influence.

Avoid actions that risk a military confrontation with the Soviet Union. The United States paid homage to independence for the Baltic republics of the Soviet Union and provided token support for Tibetan nationalists in their claims against the People's Republic of China. However, because of the need to minimize the possibility of war or political crisis with the Soviet Union or the Sino-Soviet bloc, nothing more was done to buttress these claims.

Preserve the existing state. The breakup of a state into its ethnic components, it was feared, could increase the risk of armed conflict and destabilize other multiethnic states. Not only did the United States favor the preservation of existing states, it also favored the integration of a number of states into multilateral groupings, such as the European Community. In fact, support for one trend reinforced support for the other, for the building blocks for integration were themselves states of some ethnic diversity.

Resist changes in the international boundaries established after World War II. A number of the borders established after World War II, both in Europe and in the former colonial areas, were fragile and arbitrary. U.S. officials—as well as those of other governments—feared that any change in those borders could stimulate demands for independence or alteration of boundaries by other groups seeking self-determination and threaten stability. This view dominated the Organization of African Unity, which strongly opposed territorial adjustments of the former colonial territories in Africa. Thus while official policy supported border changes to correct certain anomalies from World War II—such as the unification of Germany—in practice, the U.S. government found many strategic reasons to preserve the status quo, whatever the merits of individual claims.

Gauge the domestic political response. Particularly during and after the Vietnam War, any commitment of American resources, armed forces, or diplomatic capital in foreign adventures where the outcomes and even the aims were dubious was highly unpopular. Foreign liberation movements and separatist groups rarely attracted any sizable American constituency. The only exceptions were conflicts that were seen as part of the confrontation with the Soviet Union, including the four regional conflicts that defined the controversial Reagan Doctrine of the 1980s: Afghanistan, Angola, Cambodia, and Nicaragua.[1]

---

[1] See Louis Henkin et al., *Right v. Might*, 2d ed. (New York: Council on Foreign Relations, 1991), pp. 1–36.

The International Response

D uring the Cold War period, the rest of the international community was as reluctant as the United States to support secessionist demands. Indeed, prior to its recognition of the states emerging from the disintegration of the Soviet Union and of Yugoslavia, the international community accepted only one full-fledged secessionist claim since 1945: that of Bangladesh in 1971.[2]

The international response to two secessionist conflicts in Africa during the 1960s underscores the dilemmas and challenges posed by separatist demands and the skepticism with which such claims were met by the international community.

The province of Katanga's declaration of independence from the Congo in July 1960—shortly after the Congo itself was granted independence from Belgium—prompted an armed conflict that lasted until January 1963. U.N. Security Council resolutions during the initial months of the crisis reflected a view that the U.N. role was to restore order but remain neutral on the question of Katanga's ultimate political status. In November 1961, however, the Security Council rejected Katanga's claim to independence, passing a resolution condemning "secessionist activities and armed action now being carried on by the provincial administration of Katanga with the aid of external resources and foreign mercenaries, and *completely rejecting* the claim that Katanga is a 'sovereign independent nation.'"[3]

The U.N. position reflected a number of concerns on the part of member states. A primary concern was that the survival of Katanga as an independent state could set a dangerous precedent undermining the political unity of other African countries. It was largely pressure from African states that led

---

[2]A form of "secession" also occurred in the British trust territory of Cameroon, when the United Nations arranged for two separate plebiscite areas that could choose independence through joining either French Cameroun or Nigeria. The northern province of the British territory was permitted to separate and join Nigeria, while the rest of the territory joined French Cameroun. The new Republic of Cameroon then went to the International Court of Justice to nullify the merger of the northern province to Nigeria, but the Court rejected the case as moot because of the decision of the U.N. General Assembly approving the merger as a consequence of the U.N.-supervised plebiscite. *Northern Cameroons (Cameroon v. United Kingdom)*, ICJ REPORTS 1963, p. 15.

[3]U.N. Sec. Council Res. 169 (XVI), November 24, 1961, 9:0. Emphasis in original.

to Security Council resolutions in February and November 1961 authorizing the use of force by the United Nations to end the secession.[4] Other concerns included fear that the secession of Katanga—the Congo's wealthiest
province—would have disastrous economic consequences for the Congo,
and suspicion on the part of a number of Third World states that Belgium
(which had intervened early in the conflict on behalf of Katanga) and its
allies were supporting secession to protect business interests in the region.[5]

The international community also refused to support attempts by the
Ibos of the eastern region of Nigeria to create the independent Republic of
Biafra in May 1967.[6] In the three-year conflict that followed, the United
Nations and the Organization of African Unity consistently supported the
territorial integrity of Nigeria, despite popular sympathy for the plight of
the Ibo people. There was some dissent from this policy. Four African
states—Gabon, the Ivory Coast, Tanzania, and Zambia—recognized Biafra
and provided material support. A handful of other states provided humanitarian assistance and some arms to the Ibos.[7]

The fact that a well-defined group, the victim of communal riots outside of its traditional homeland, sought sanctuary by breaking away led many
Americans, including a number of government officials, to believe that the
effort deserved U.S. support. Indeed, the U.S. government was not unequivocal in its opposition to Biafran independence. However, in the end, the
importance the United States attributed to Nigeria as a regional power and
the traditional fear of the consequences of even one border change—particularly in Africa—were too strong. Officially, the United States maintained
a position of neutrality, refusing to sell arms to the Nigerian government

---

[4]Heather Wilson, *International Law and the Use of Force by National Liberation Movements*
(Oxford: Clarendon Press, 1988), p. 84; Anthony Verrier, *International Peacekeeping: United Nations Forces in a Troubled World* (New York: Penguin, 1981), p. 67.

[5]Lee C. Buchheit, *Secession: The Legitimacy of Self-Determination* (New Haven: Yale University
Press, 1978), pp. 142 and 152.

[6]See H. Wilson, pp. 85–97; Buchheit, pp. 162–76; John J. Stremlau, *The International Politics of the Nigerian Civil War (1967–1970)* (Princeton: Princeton University Press, 1977).

[7]Alexis Heraclides, "Secessionist Minorities and External Involvement," *International Organization*, vol. 44 (Summer 1990), p. 348. Some commentators have suggested, however, that this
departure from international practice reflected neither a desire for a Biafran victory nor support
for the principle of self-determination, but rather a desire for the destabilization of Nigeria. See,
for example, John de St. Jorré, *The Nigerian Civil War* (London: Hodder and Stoughton, 1972),
pp. 193–4.

and, at the same time, shying away from recognizing Biafran independence. But it basically supported a unified Nigeria.

Indeed, the position of most states on the conflict was in line with that of the United Nations, summed up by U.N. secretary-general U Thant: "The United Nations' attitude is unequivocal. As an international organization, the United Nations has never accepted and does not accept and I do not believe it will ever accept the principle of secession of a part of its Member State."[8]

Bangladesh stands as the dramatic exception where, in the end, the international community accepted a secessionist movement. A number of features distinguish the case of Bangladesh—formerly East Pakistan—from that of Katanga or Biafra and help explain the different response.

With the partition of the Indian subcontinent in 1947, Pakistan was formed out of the Muslim states in the northwest and the province of East Bengal in the east. More than a thousand miles separated West and East Pakistan. The inhabitants of East Pakistan were ethnically and culturally distinct from West Pakistanis; moreover, because of unequal economic and political treatment, East Pakistan was underdeveloped in comparison to the West.[9] A crisis developed in late 1970 and early 1971, when negotiations between West and East Pakistani leaders over a new constitution broke down. By March 1971, West Pakistan had built up its armed presence and begun a brutal campaign against the separatists in the East. The crisis eventually brought Indian intervention on behalf of East Pakistan and a full-scale war between India and Pakistan.

The United Nations was slow to act. Only after India and Pakistan were locked in conflict did the U.N. Security Council and General Assembly address the situation.[10] The international community's ultimate recognition of Bangladesh did not signal acceptance of any general right of secession, even in the case of unrepresentative or oppressive government. It is

---

[8] Press Conference at Dakar, Senegal, January 4, 1970. Reprinted in *U.N. Monthly Chronicle*, vol. 7 (February 1970), p. 36. U Thant's statement, as well as his procrastination in presenting the Bangladesh case to the Security Council, may have reflected the fact that his home country, Burma, had been (and remains) plagued by secessionist movements.

[9] Buchheit, p. 201.

[10] Various Security Council resolutions on Bangladesh were vetoed by the Soviet Union, which at that time usually protected India against an unfavorable decision, while India defended the Soviet Union in the General Assembly when the majority opposed its actions (for example, during the Hungarian crisis in 1956).

impossible to isolate the merits of the case for secession in Bangladesh from two critical factors that influenced the world community's decision to recognize statehood: the enormous brutality of the West Pakistani army and an Indian intervention that seemed to make independence inevitable.[11]

The Law of Self-Determination

I nternational law in the post-war period also supported a narrow application of the principle of self-determination except toward claims of a clearly anti-colonial character. That limited application stemmed at least in part from confusion and controversy over the meaning and scope of "self-determination" during and after World War I, when the concept was popularized by President Woodrow Wilson.

The Wilsonian Era

Although the notion of self-determination can be traced back to the American Revolution,[12] Wilson was the concept's most famous proponent. His use of the term, however, was at times imprecise and inconsistent. As one commentator put it, analyzing "the various strands of Wilsonian prewar, wartime, and postwar thought on self-determination reveals a fusion and confusion of several ideas."[13]

For example, the term "self-determination" came to be associated with two distinctly different concepts. The first, known as "external self-determination," was that people have the right to choose their own sovereignty—that is, to be free from external coercion or alien domination. Wilson embraced this notion when, in identifying American war aims in 1917, he spoke of upholding "the liberty, the self-government, and the undictated

---

[11]Buchheit, p. 213.

[12]The fathers of the American Revolution often cited Holland's successful rebellion against Spain in the late 16th century as an inspiration for their own revolt. Other successful acts of self-determination included the Greek revolt against Ottoman rule in the 1820s and Belgium's secession from the Kingdom of the Netherlands in 1830. Unsuccessful acts of self-determination included Poland's rebellion against Russian rule in 1830–31 and the Hungarian uprising against Hapsburg rule in 1848, both of which found strong sympathy in the United States.

[13]Michla Pomerance, "The United States and Self-Determination: Perspectives on the Wilsonian Conception," *American Journal of International Law*, vol. 70 (1976), p. 20.

development of all peoples. . . . No people must be forced under sovereignty under which it does not wish to live. No territory must change hands except for the purpose of securing those who inhabit it a fair chance of life and liberty."[14]

The second concept was that people have the right to meaningful participation in the political process. Only through such participation could people choose their own social order and form of government—thus fully exercising a right to "internal self-determination."[15]

At the 1919 Paris Peace Conference, various delegations sought to discredit the concept of self-determination by giving the term its most extreme meaning—implying a right to political independence for every ethnic group no matter how small. Wilson's own secretary of state, Robert Lansing, was highly critical of Wilson's embrace of the principle of self-determination. In his notes at the Peace Conference, he wrote:

> The more I think about the President's declaration as to the right of 'self-determination,' the more convinced I am of the danger of putting such ideas into the minds of certain races. It is bound to be the basis of impossible demands on the Peace Congress and create trouble in many lands. . . . Will it not breed discontent, disorder, and rebellion? . . . The phrase is simply loaded with dynamite. It will raise hopes which can never be realized. It will, I fear, cost thousands of lives. In the end it is bound to be discredited, to be called the dream of an idealist who failed to realize the danger until too late to check those who attempt to put the principle in force. What a calamity that the phrase was ever uttered! What misery it will cause![16]

Although Wilson underestimated the complexities of applying the principle of self-determination after World War I, it is clear that opponents of

---

[14]Message from President Wilson to Russia, June 9, 1917. Reprinted in *Official Statements of War Aims and Peace Proposals, December 1916 to November 1918*, ed. James B. Scott (Washington, D.C.: Carnegie Endowment for International Peace, 1921), pp. 104–5.

[15]Michla Pomerance, *Self-Determination in Law and Practice* (Boston: Martinus Nijhoff Publishers, 1982), p. 1; Hurst Hannum, *Autonomy, Sovereignty, and Self-Determination: The Accommodation of Conflicting Rights* (Philadelphia: University of Pennsylvania Press, 1990), p. 30.

[16]Robert Lansing, *The Peace Negotiations: A Personal Narrative* (Boston: Houghton Mifflin Company, 1921), pp. 97–98.

the principle interpreted it in a way that Wilson did not intend. Wilson did not contend that independent statehood was the only outcome consistent with an exercise of the right to self-determination. Nor did ethnic boundaries, in Wilson's opinion, have to coincide with new political boundaries. He held that people should be permitted to choose their own sovereignty (most often as part of or added to an existing state) and should not be "bartered about from sovereignty to sovereignty as if they were mere chattels and pawns in a game." The "self" in self-determination did not necessarily have to coincide with an ethnic group. As Michla Pomerance has argued, in Wilson's version of the principle "it was still not clear that the 'self' which was to free itself from 'alien' rule was synonymous with the 'nation.' Self-determination did not necessarily require the coincidence, in so far as possible, of the ethnographic and political maps."[17]

In the aftermath of World War I, neither the external nor the internal promises of the principle of self-determination were fulfilled. Wilson's fellow peacemakers stood by the principle in rhetoric at the Paris Peace Conference, but rarely put it into practice. In part, the difficulty stemmed from conceptual problems with the principle itself. The most obvious question was how to identify a "self" that held the right to self-determination. Were ethnic or territorial criteria more relevant? If significant population movements had taken place, how were the rights of the historical populations to be weighed against those of the present population? Once a population with a right to self-determination had been identified, how were its wishes to be determined?

The larger problem, however, was that the Great Powers discarded the principle to create what they perceived to be economically and strategically viable states—states capable of counter-balancing Germany and Soviet Russia. In the demarcation of Hungary's boundaries, the ultimate settlement was based not on ethnic considerations, but on the demands of Romania, Serbia, and Czech and Slovak nationalist leaders living in exile, whose participation in the war had been secured by promises of territory. The result was an array of states, new and old, with large and often discontented minorities.[18] While

---

[17]Pomerance, "Perspectives on the Wilsonian Conception," p. 18.

[18]See, for example, Robin Oakley, *Eastern Europe, 1740–1985: Feudalism to Communism* (Minneapolis: University of Minnesota Press, 1986), pp. 158–61; Stephen D. Kertesz, "The Consequences of World War I: The Effects on East Central Europe," reprinted in *Essays on World War I: A Case Study on Trianon*, ed. Béla K. Király, Peter Pastor, and Ivan Sanders (Highland Lakes, New Jersey: Atlantic Research and Publications, 1982), pp. 47–48.

a number of plebiscites were held—including in Upper Silesia, Schleswig, and the Saar—they were reserved for certain disputed frontier regions, and were not applied to more controversial areas like the Sudetenland or South Tyrol. Indeed, none of the successor states created at Versailles were established by plebiscite.[19] The Great Powers also did not apply the principle of self-determination to their own people. Nor did they respect ethnic boundaries beyond Europe—either as they divided Germany's vast Asian and African territories or in their own colonial empires.

That self-determination in the inter-war period was a principle with only limited application is well illustrated by the League of Nations' handling of a dispute over part of Finland known as the Aaland Islands. In 1920 at the Paris Peace Conference, representatives of the Aaland Islands formally requested annexation to Sweden. The International Committee of Jurists, charged with presenting the League of Nations with an advisory opinion on the matter, noted,

> Although the principle of self-determination of peoples plays an important part in modern political thought. . . there is no mention of it in the covenant of the League of Nations. The recognition of this principle in a certain number of international treaties cannot be considered as sufficient to put it on the same footing as a positive rule of the Law of Nations.[20]

The Committee regarded Finland, which had achieved its own independence from Russia in 1917, as a definitely constituted state rather than as a state or territory in turmoil. This calculation made all the difference, for it effectively tied the Committee's hands on the question of secession for the Aaland Islands. In a definitely constituted state, the right of self-determination was limited to less radical options. Thus the Aaland population was denied its preference to join Sweden. However, a special Commission of Rapporteurs was established by the Council of the League of Nations to "establish conditions favorable to the maintenance of Peace in that part of the world." The Commission refused to separate the islands from Finland, but recommended autonomy for the islands, under an international guarantee, and

---

[19]H. Wilson, p. 57; Pomerance, *Self-Determination*, p. 4.

[20]Report of the International Committee of Jurists, *League of Nations Official Journal*, Special Supplement 3 (October 1920), p. 5.

demilitarization of the archipelago. Significantly, only Finnish citizens already legally residing on the islands were permitted to purchase real estate there and obtain good title. Thus the secessionist movement emerged from the process deprived of union with Sweden but with greater local autonomy within the Finnish state.

The Era of Decolonization

From a doctrine narrowly applied after World War I when the Great Powers redrew European boundaries, self-determination in international law evolved into an enforceable right to freedom from colonial rule. The shift was gradual. Self-determination was not immediately recognized as a fundamental "right" of the U.N. scheme established in 1945. Articles 1(2) and 55 of the U.N. Charter explicitly refer to "self-determination of peoples," but the concept is treated as a "principle" rather than a "right."[21]

The more enforceable character that the principle of self-determination attained during the era of decolonization was rooted in Chapters XI and XII of the U.N. Charter on non-self-governing and trust territories. Neither chapter contains an explicit reference to "self-determination," but each establishes the principle indirectly. Article 73 of Chapter XI calls upon states administering non-self-governing territories—that is, territories "whose peoples have not yet attained a full measure of self-government"—to promote "self-government, to take due account of the political aspirations of the peoples, and to assist them in the progressive development of their free political institutions." Article 76 of Chapter XII states that a basic objective of the U.N. trusteeship system is to promote "progressive development" in the trust territories "towards self-government or independence."

A critical aspect of each chapter was its focus on territory rather than ethnicity. Progress toward self-government was to be promoted in non-self-governing and trust territories as whole political entities—regardless of any internal ethnic, linguistic, or religious divisions. In effect, colonial boundaries were to function as the boundaries of emerging states. The emphasis on territory rather than ethnicity limited the "self" that was entitled to move toward self-government. It also foreshadowed future tension between the

---

[21]Article 1(2) places the principle among the purposes of the United Nations, while Article 55 refers to the principle before listing social, political, and economic goals that the United Nations shall promote.

principle of self-determination and the competing principle of territorial integrity, which worked to prevent the extension of a right of self-determination to ethnic groups or minorities within territories administered as a single unit by a colonial power.

In the early years of the United Nations, members split on matters related to self-determination and decolonization. While East European and Asian countries supported a broad interpretation of the principle, Western countries hesitated to promote international involvement in what they considered domestic matters or to support a concept they feared could be applied to groups within their own territories.[22] In 1952, a resolution calling upon members of the United Nations to "recognize and promote the realization of the right of self-determination of the peoples of Non-Self-Governing and Trust Territories" passed by a vote of 40 to 14, with 6 abstentions.[23] Eight years later, the admission of newly independent states to the United Nations had significantly altered the body's composition, giving powerful momentum to the development of a right to self-determination. On December 14, 1960, by a vote of 89 to 0, with 9 abstentions, the General Assembly passed a landmark resolution on decolonization. Known as the Declaration on the Granting of Independence to Colonial Territories and Countries, Resolution 1514 states that "All peoples have the right to self-determination; by virtue of that right they freely determine their political status and freely pursue their economic, social, and cultural development."[24]

While they were divided in their depth of support for anti-colonial self-determination, the nations of the world were united in their opposition to other self-determination movements. Former colonies were as vulnerable to secessionists as were their colonial masters. The decolonization resolution, therefore, also stresses the preservation of territorial integrity, by stating that "Any attempt aimed at the partial or total disruption of the national unity and the territorial integrity of a country is incompatible with the purposes and principles of the Charter of the United Nations."

---

[22]H. Wilson, p. 61.

[23]U.N.G.A. Res. 637A (VII), December 16, 1952, 40:14:6. Voting against were Austria, Belgium, Canada, Denmark, France, Iceland, Luxembourg, the Netherlands, New Zealand, Norway, Sweden, South Africa, the United Kingdom, and the United States. Abstaining were Ecuador, Israel, Nicaragua, Paraguay, Thailand, and Turkey.

[24]U.N.G.A. Res. 1514 (XV), December 14, 1960, 89:0:9. Austria, Belgium, the Dominican Republic, France, Portugal, Spain, South Africa, the United Kingdom, and the United States abstained.

Resolution 1541, adopted the following day, reflected both an attempt to uphold the principle of territorial integrity and to limit the "self" to whom the principle of self-determination could apply. The resolution specifies that a territory would be considered "non-self-governing" under Chapter XI of the U.N. Charter only if it were both "geographically separate" and "distinct ethnically and/or culturally from the country administering it." Thus, strictly read, Resolution 1541 rules out classifying a minority or ethnic group on a state's territory as a "non-self-governing" entity entitled to self-determination or self-government.[25] These dual requirements of ethnic and geographic distinctiveness came to be known as the theory of "salt-water" colonialism.[26]

The year 1960 marked a clear turning point in the development of the right to self-determination in international law in the colonial context. After 1960, the right of colonial peoples to self-determination and independence was reaffirmed almost annually by the General Assembly.[27]

The adoption in 1966 of two international human rights covenants—one on economic, social, and cultural rights, the other on civil and political rights—raised the possibility that international law might provide some support for other forms of self-determination.[28] Article I of both covenants states, "All peoples have the right of self-determination. By virtue of the right they freely determine their political status and freely pursue their economic, social, and cultural development." This language, however, remained open to interpretation. India, for example, lodged a reservation restricting the applicability of the right of self-determination "only to the peoples under foreign domination" and not "to sovereign independent States or to a section of a people or nation—which is the essence of national integrity." The

---

[25]U.N.G.A. Res. 1541 (XV), December 15, 1960, 69:2:21.

[26]See Patrick Thornberry, *International Law and the Rights of Minorities* (Oxford: Clarendon Press, 1991), p. 17.

[27]H. Wilson, p. 70.

[28]International Covenant on Economic, Social and Cultural Rights, U.N.G.A. Res. 2200 (XXI), adopted December 16, 1966, and entered into force January 3, 1976; International Covenant on Civil and Political Rights, U.N.G.A. Res. 2200A (XXI), adopted December 16, 1966, and entered into force March 23, 1976. For an analysis of the evolution of the relevant U.N. resolutions and the Covenants' provision, see Antonio Cassesse, "The Self-Determination of Peoples," in *The International Bill of Rights: The Covenant on Civil and Political Rights*, ed. Louis Henkin (New York: Columbia University Press, 1981), pp. 92–113.

Netherlands objected to India's reservation, arguing that "the right of self-determination as embodied in the covenant is conferred upon all peoples." France and the Federal Republic of Germany objected on similar grounds.[29]

The situation was further muddled in 1970, when the General Assembly unanimously approved Resolution 2625, known as the Declaration on Principles of International Law concerning Friendly Relations and Co-operation among States.[30] The Declaration expands the scope of the right to self-determination, arguing that it can be implemented through the "establishment of a sovereign and independent State, the free association with an independent State or the emergence into any other political status freely determined by a people."

Like the critical texts on self-determination that preceded it, the Declaration on Friendly Relations emphasizes the preservation of territorial integrity, stating that its affirmation of the right of self-determination should not be construed as "authorizing or encouraging any action which would dismember or impair, totally or in part, the territorial integrity or political unity of sovereign and independent States." But the Declaration contains a qualification that distinguishes it from previous resolutions on self-determination: It specifies that the protection of territorial integrity applies to states "possessed of a government representing the whole people belonging to the territory without distinction as to race, creed or colour."

There is no consensus among scholars or governments on how this qualification affects the relationship between the right of self-determination and the principle of territorial integrity. Several commentators have argued that the principle of self-determination can be accorded priority over the competing principle of territorial integrity if a state is not "possessed of a government representing the whole people."[31] One author suggests that the

---

[29]Centre for Human Rights, *Human Rights: Status of International Instruments* (New York: United Nations, 1987), p. 9.

[30]U.N.G.A. Res. 2625 (XXV), October 24, 1970, unanimous. The 1970 Declaration codified several earlier resolutions that pioneered the concepts discussed in this paragraph, starting with U.N.G.A. Resolutions 567 (VII) of 1952 and 1467 (XIV) of 1959. See Louis B. Sohn, "The Concept of Autonomy in International Law and the Practice of the United Nations," *Israel Law Review*, vol. 15 (1980), pp. 180–90; Sohn, "Models of Autonomy within the United Nations Framework," in *Models of Autonomy*, ed. Yoram Dinstein (New Brunswick, New Jersey: Transaction Books, 1981), pp. 5–22.

[31]See, for example, Ved P. Nanda, "Self-Determination Under International Law: Validity of Claims to Secede," *Case Western Reserve Journal of International Law*, vol. 13 (1981), p. 269; Robert Rosenstock, "The Declaration of International Law concerning Friendly Relations: A Survey," *American Journal of International Law*, vol. 65 (1971), p. 732.

provision "constitutes an unambiguous affirmation of the applicability of the right of self-determination to peoples inside the political boundaries of existing sovereign and independent states in situations where the government does not represent the governed."[32] This interpretation seems to create a category of "peoples" possessing a right of self-determination outside the colonial context.

Other commentators view the Declaration on Friendly Relations as having far less sweeping implications. Noting that the requirement of "representative government" appears in a *racial* context, they argue that the principle of territorial integrity is superseded by that of self-determination only in the case of racist regimes. "Only pariah States like South Africa, which oppresses its majority on racial grounds, are likely to be affected. . . . 'Whole' territories or peoples are the focus of rights, rather than ethnic groups."[33]

Thus while there is no doubt that there is an international legal right of self-determination in the context of decolonization, the extension of that right to non-colonial situations was not clear as the Cold War came to an end. Most scholars and governments had concluded that the principle of political unity prevailed over any expression of self-determination within a state. As one author has noted, the international community "subscribes to a highly conventional interpretation of the principle of national self-determination. It cannot be invoked—at least not with any hope of securing widespread support—by disaffected minorities within states."[34] However, we discuss in Chapter Four developments in international law, including the protection of minority rights, that are beginning to chip away at the conventional interpretation.

---

[32]M.G. Kaldharan Nayar, "Self-Determination beyond the Colonial Context: Biafra in Retrospect," *Texas International Law Journal*, vol. 10 (1975), p. 337.

[33]Patrick Thornberry, "Self-Determination, Minorities, Human Rights: A Review of International Instruments," *International Comparative Law Quarterly*, vol. 38 (October 1989), p. 877. See also Pomerance, *Self-Determination*, p. 39; Antonio Cassese, "The Helsinki Declaration and Self-Determination," in *Human Rights, International Law and the Helsinki Accord*, ed. Thomas Buergenthal (New York: Universe Books, 1977), p. 90. Draft proposals by the United States and the United Kingdom each stated that a government had to represent "all distinct peoples" within its territory; a draft by Czechoslovakia and others made a similar point. The rejection of these drafts is indicative of the international community's unwillingness to grant to groups within states a right to self-determination that could take precedence over the principle of territorial integrity. See Thornberry, "Self-Determination," p. 876.

[34]James Mayall, "Non-Intervention, Self-Determination and the 'New World Order,' " *International Affairs*, vol. 67 (1991), p. 424.

A few analysts have argued that the potential for international recognition of a right of secession for a self-determination movement can be found in other aspects of international law. Some authors have argued that such a right can arise when a central government engages in "internal colonization," creating a situation in which people in a distinct geographic area effectively become "non-self-governing" with respect to the rest of the state.[35] James Crawford notes that Resolution 1541 states that a non-self-governing region is one that is both geographically and ethnically distinct. While geographic separateness has generally been taken to mean separation across land or sea, "there is no good reason why other defining characteristics, including historical boundaries or *de facto* boundaries established through the hostile action of the government in question, might not also be relevant."[36]

Events in Yugoslavia and the Soviet Union at the close of the Cold War forced the international community to cope with the demands of groups seeking to break off from existing states. International law, with its traditional rejection of such claims, provided little guidance. As the next chapter demonstrates, the United States and the international community scrambled to respond, with decidedly mixed results.

---

[35]H. Wilson, p. 82; James Crawford, "Self-Determination outside the Colonial Context," in *Self-Determination in the Commonwealth*, ed. W.J. Allan Macartney (Aberdeen: Aberdeen University Press, 1988), p. 13.

[36]Crawford, p. 13.

Chapter Two

POST-COLD WAR POLICY:
THREE CASES

D ramatic events accompanying the end of the Cold War—the peaceful breakup of the Soviet Union, the violent splintering of Yugoslavia, the brutal suppression of the Kurds and Shia in Iraq—compelled the international community to deal with the consequences of self-determination claims. In this chapter, we briefly review the U.S. and international reactions to these three events, since they provide a point of reference for our proposals for how the international community should respond.

The first two principles guiding U.S. policy during the Cold War, which focused on containing the Soviet Union while avoiding a war with the Soviet bloc, were rendered obsolete with the disintegration of the Soviet empire. The other principles—support for existing states and borders and avoidance of overseas commitments—continue to influence U.S. policy. A brief survey of the U.S. and international responses to crises involving self-determination claims since the end of the Cold War shows how inadequate the principles that previously guided U.S. policy and the norms of international law are now. The United States has had great difficulty adjusting to the reality of self-determination claims, and particularly to the fact that some may lead to secession.

The Breakup of the Soviet Union

M ore than twenty months passed from the time the Baltic republics of the Soviet Union took initial steps toward independence until the country was formally dissolved. U.S. policy toward the Baltics set a pattern that would be followed until shortly before the Soviet Union's dissolution. Rather than providing rhetorical support for moves toward sovereignty and independence among the various republics or weighing each claim on its merits, the United States adopted a "wait-and-see" approach as a means to a larger political objective: the survival of Soviet president Mikhail Gorbachev in a mostly unified Soviet Union.

The case of Lithuania is instructive. While the United States consistently reiterated support for the right of Lithuania to one day be free again, it never acted to further that objective. The United States had had diplomatic relations with Lithuania in the 1920s and 1930s, had never recognized Stalin's annexation in 1940, had only suspended treaty relations with Lithuania, and had permitted a Lithuanian diplomatic presence in Washington, D.C., throughout the Cold War. Nonetheless, when Lithuania moved toward independence in early 1990,[1] the United States tilted toward Moscow.

On March 12, 1990, one day after Lithuania declared its independence, State Department spokesperson Margaret Tutwiler outlined a rationale underpinning the U.S. decision not to recognize the Lithuanian government: "U.S. practice has been to establish formal relations with the lawful government of a state once that government is in effective control of its territory and capable of entering into and fulfilling international obligations. When we are satisfied that the Lithuanian government can meet these requirements, we will establish formal diplomatic relations."[2] Yet how could the Lithuanian government meet the requirements if the United States and other major powers were, in effect, strengthening Gorbachev's hand by responding so tepidly to Lithuanian aspirations? Were there no diplomatic moves that could have shown more sympathy and encouragement for the Lithuanian claim to self-determination?[3]

---

[1]Lithuania's newly elected parliament declared the republic's independence on March 11, 1990. Moscow responded with an economic embargo as well as a campaign of intimidation, sending a convoy of tanks through Vilnius and beating up Lithuanian youths who had deserted the Soviet army as a protest against Soviet rule. For a discussion of events in Lithuania and the Soviet nationality issue more generally, see Martha Brill Olcott, "The Slide into Disunion," *Current History*, vol. 90 (October 1991), pp. 338–44.

[2]State Department Regular Briefing, March 12, 1990, Federal News Service Transcript, S-1-3, p. 2.

[3]See David J. Scheffer, "A Way to Save Lithuania," *New York Times*, March 28, 1990, p. A29.

The reluctance to move toward recognition of an independent government in Lithuania continued for nearly a year and a half. A day before a treaty between Gorbachev and the leaders of nine non-Baltic republics on a more decentralized Soviet Union was to be signed, hard-line Soviet leaders launched an unsuccessful coup. In the aftermath, all three Baltic republics reasserted their independence. But the United States stood back while European governments took the lead in responding to their claims. Daily political calculations became all-important. The United States knew that the Baltics did not need early U.S. recognition after the coup in order to achieve real independence, and gave priority to its long-term relations with what would remain of the Soviet Union. The United States sought to avoid the appearance of a victorious rival hastening the Soviet Union's breakup.

The Baltics' achievement of independence after the August 1991 aborted coup in Moscow can obscure the fact that U.S. policy at no point really advanced—and may have retarded—the cause of independence for the Baltics. In the critical period between March 1990 and August 1991, Washington gambled on Gorbachev, fearing that Baltic secession might erode his power base in the Soviet government and perhaps accelerate the drive of other republics to secede.

Such caution was not an anomaly in U.S. policy. On August 1, 1991, weeks before the failed coup in Moscow, President Bush delivered an important statement in Kiev, Ukraine, on U.S. policy toward the Soviet Union and self-determination claims within it. Warning against "suicidal nationalism" in the republics, he stated that the United States would "maintain the strongest possible relationship with the Soviet Government."[4] His statements came at a time when many astute observers felt that Ukraine was destined to be an independent state and that the Soviet government did not have the power to stop it.

The failed coup and the independence of the Baltic states nudged the United States into formulating a number of "basic principles" that would govern U.S. policy toward the remainder of the Soviet Union. Set forth by

---

[4]Remarks to the Supreme Soviet of the Republic of the Ukraine in Kiev, Soviet Union, August 1, 1991. Reprinted in *Weekly Compilation of Presidential Documents*, vol. 27 (1991), p. 1094. See also Brent Scowcroft, "Bush Got It Right in the Soviet Union," *New York Times*, August 18, 1991, sec. 4, p. 15.

Secretary of State James Baker on September 4, 1991, these principles called upon Soviet leaders and leaders of the republics to:

a) support internationally accepted principles, including democratic values and practices and the principles of the Helsinki Final Act;
b) respect existing borders, both internal and external, with change through peaceful and consensual means consistent with the principles of the Conference on Security and Cooperation in Europe (CSCE);
c) support the rule of law and democratic processes;
d) safeguard human rights, including minority rights; and
e) respect international law and obligations, especially the provisions of the Helsinki Final Act and the Charter of Paris.[5]

These principles were not posited as criteria that, if adhered to by republics seeking international recognition as independent states, would bring U.S. recognition. Rather, they were to govern the U.S. approach to change within the Soviet Union—regardless of whether that change brought a new type of union or the disintegration of the state.

As the breakup of the Soviet Union appeared more likely throughout the fall of 1991, with Gorbachev failing to secure the agreement of republic leaders to a renewed union treaty, the United States shifted its policy. Shortly before Ukraine's referendum on independent statehood in December 1991, the United States announced that it would move "expeditiously" to recognize Ukraine if the referendum passed.[6] After the voters supported independence by an overwhelming majority, the United States laid out "considerations" that would govern the pace of formal diplomatic ties. In addition to the general September 4 principles, the United States called upon Ukraine to:

a) take steps to ensure safe, responsible, and reliable control of nuclear weapons; to prevent proliferation of dangerous military-related technology; and to support implementation of the relevant international agreements, including the Strategic Arms Reduction Treaty (START),

---

[5]"U.S. Approach to Changes in the Soviet Union." Reprinted in U.S. *Department of State Dispatch*, vol. 2 (1991), p. 667.

[6]"U.S., Turning from Moscow, Would Grant Recognition to an Independent Ukraine," *New York Times*, November 28, 1991, p. A1.

the Conventional Forces in Europe (CFE) treaty, the Nuclear Non-Proliferation Treaty (NPT), and the Biological Weapons Convention;

b) demonstrate a commitment to economic policies aimed at facilitating free markets and free and fair trade, both with other republics and with the international community more generally; and

c) take responsibility for a fair share of the Soviet Union's external debt.[7]

These considerations and the September 4 principles were ultimately woven together as the basis for an overall approach to self-determination claims by the Soviet republics. This approach was outlined by Secretary Baker in a December 12 speech at Princeton University, in which he called upon all republics to commit to responsible security policies, free trade, free-market economics, and democratic political practices.[8] This was four days after Russian president Boris Yeltsin, Ukrainian president Leonid Kravchuk, and Belarussian prime minister Stanislav Shushkevich met in Minsk, Belarus, and declared the formation of a new "commonwealth" and the dissolution of the Soviet Union. Thus, only after it was clear that the Soviet Union would not survive did the United States accept and act upon this reality.

Following the resignation of Soviet president Mikhail Gorbachev and formal dissolution of the Soviet government on December 25, the United States announced recognition of the twelve remaining Soviet republics as independent states. The United States proposed establishing full diplomatic relations with only six of the new states: Armenia, Belarus, Kazakhstan, Kyrgyzstan, Russia, and Ukraine—states that the administration claimed had made specific commitments to responsible security policies and democratic principles.

Despite Baker's articulation of principles guiding the pace of U.S. recognition, U.S. policy at times seemed governed more by political expedience. The fact that all four successor states that possessed strategic nuclear weapons—Belarus, Kazakhstan, Russia, and Ukraine—were among the first states to win U.S. recognition risked sending a dangerous message—that

---

[7]White House Regular Briefing, December 2, 1991, Federal News Service Transcript, W-1-1, p. 1.

[8]"America and the Collapse of the Soviet Empire: What Has to be Done." Reprinted in *U.S. Department of State Dispatch*, vol. 2 (1991), pp. 887–93; "Baker Presents Steps to Aid Transition by Soviets," *New York Times*, December 13, 1991, p. A1.

retaining nuclear weapons would offer the new states leverage with the West. Furthermore, the recognition of Armenia but not Azerbaijan may have exacerbated tensions in the disputed territory of Nagorno-Karabakh—populated by Armenians but located in and administered by Azerbaijan—by undermining a purportedly neutral U.S. position on the conflict.[9] Concern—however inflated—that a policy of selective recognition could prompt the Islamic republics of Tajikistan, Turkmenistan, and Uzbekistan in Central Asia and Azerbaijan in the Caucasus to turn toward Iran prompted the United States to quickly secure pro forma promises on democratic principles and to establish diplomatic ties.

By February 19, 1992, the United States had granted formal diplomatic recognition to eleven of the twelve non-Baltic republics.[10] Recognition of the government of the final republic, Georgia, was granted on March 24, 1992, after its civil war subsided and commitments were received from its new leader, former Soviet foreign minister Eduard Shevardnadze.[11]

The Yugoslav Crisis

Caution, inconsistencies, and short-term considerations also characterized the American and, to a lesser degree, the European Community's initial responses to Yugoslavia's self-determination crisis. Until hostilities broke out in mid-1991, the United States and European governments asserted unconditional support for Yugoslav unity. That policy, at least in part, reflected concern that any splintering of Yugoslavia would be violent.

When Serbia's strongly nationalist president, Slobodan Milošević, began campaigning for a stronger Yugoslav federal center, calls among Slovenes,

---

[9]See, for example, Paul A. Goble, "Forget the Soviet Union," *Foreign Policy*, vol. 86 (Spring 1992), p. 64.

[10]Statement by Press Secretary Fitzwater on the President's Meeting with President Mircea Snegur of Moldova, February 18, 1992. Reprinted in *Weekly Compilation of Presidential Documents*, vol. 28 (1992), p. 292; Statement by Press Secretary Fitzwater on Establishment of Diplomatic Relations with Azerbaijan, Tajikistan, Turkmenistan, and Uzbekistan, February 19, 1992. Reprinted in *Weekly Compilation of Presidential Documents*, vol. 28 (1992), pp. 302–3.

[11]Statement by Press Secretary Fitzwater on Establishing Diplomatic Relations With Georgia, March 24, 1992. Reprinted in *Weekly Compilation of Presidential Documents*, vol. 28 (1992), pp. 542.

Croats, and Bosnians for a looser confederation or for outright secession multiplied. Slovenia, the most homogeneous of the republics, had already taken its first steps toward independence in September 1989, when its parliament approved an amendment to the republic's constitution giving it the right to secede from the Yugoslav federation. In December 1990, after 88 percent of voters favored independence, Slovenia's government set a six-month deadline for successful negotiations with other republics on a more decentralized confederation. Slovenia was joined in its demands by Croatia, whose revised December 1990 constitution included a provision that would permit a republic-wide referendum on secession upon a two-thirds vote of the parliament. Serb voters within Croatia designated their own autonomous areas and later proclaimed union with Serbia. Meanwhile, Serbia had revoked the autonomy of two of its provinces, Kosovo (with a 90 percent Albanian population) and Vojvodina (with a 19 percent Hungarian population) in September 1989, formalizing that step in September 1990 with an amendment to the Serbian constitution. In fall 1990, the U.S. Central Intelligence Agency reportedly predicted that a Yugoslav breakup would occur "most probably in the next 18 months" and called a civil war "highly likely."[12] Nevertheless, days after a May 21, 1991, referendum in which Croatia's population voted overwhelmingly to secede, the United States remained firmly committed to the "territorial integrity of Yugoslavia within its present borders."[13]

Fighting erupted in June 1991, after Croatia and Slovenia formally declared their independence. As the war in Croatia escalated throughout the summer and fall of 1991, the issue of international recognition for the Yugoslav republics became more controversial. The European Community—led on this issue by Germany—outpaced the United States. Four days after Baker's Princeton speech on the Soviet Union, the EC foreign ministers reached agreement on principles and a process for the recognition of the republics of both the Soviet Union and Yugoslavia. To gain EC recognition, the republics would have to:

a) respect the provisions of the U.N. Charter, Helsinki Final Act, and Charter of Paris, particularly with regard to the rule of law, democracy, and human rights;

---

[12]Cited in Dennison Rusinow, "Yugoslavia: Balkan Breakup?" *Foreign Policy*, vol. 83 (Summer 1991), p. 143. See also "U.S. Finds No Proof of Mass Killings at Serb Camps," *New York Times*, August 23, 1992, p. 18.

[13]Statement of May 24, 1991. Reprinted in *U.S. Department of State Dispatch*, vol. 2 (1991), p. 395.

b) establish guarantees for ethnic and minority rights;

c) respect the inviolability of borders, with change to occur only through peaceful means and by common agreement;

d) accept all relevant commitments with regard to disarmament, nuclear non-proliferation, security, and regional stability; and

e) commit to settle questions concerning state succession and regional disputes by agreement.[14]

Apart from the general criteria, the Community developed additional conditions and procedures for the Yugoslav republics. To gain recognition, the republics would have to agree to support U.N. mediation efforts and the continuation of the EC's Conference on Yugoslavia, and commit to the provisions of that Conference's draft convention. In addition, a republic seeking recognition would have to commit to adopting certain constitutional and political guarantees that it had "no territorial claims on" and "would conduct no hostile propaganda activities against" a neighboring EC state. The EC set a deadline of December 23, 1991, for the six republics to apply for recognition. An "arbitration commission" would evaluate the record of each republic on its protection of minority rights and human rights, adherence to democratic principles, and respect for existing borders. Republics found by the arbitration commission to meet the EC's conditions would be granted diplomatic recognition by the EC and its member states on January 15, 1992.

But the EC compromise accord permitted deviations from this policy. Individual EC members could confer recognition upon any republic as of January 15, even if the commission judged that it did not meet the Community's standards. Germany and Italy announced on December 19 that they would recognize Croatia and Slovenia after the republics accepted the conditions set forth by the EC and establish diplomatic relations on January 15 regardless of the EC's decision on that date. These actions underscored the somewhat disingenuous character of the EC policy. While Germany and Italy agreed to apply the EC criteria, they did not let the criteria stall or obstruct their plans to recognize Croatia and Slovenia within weeks.

---

[14]European Community, "Declaration on the Guidelines on the European Community Recognition of New States in Eastern Europe and in the Soviet Union," EPC Press Release 128/91 (December 16, 1991). For a discussion of the EC criteria and other aspects of the Yugoslav case, see Marc Weller, "The International Response to the Dissolution of the Socialist Republic of Yugoslavia," *American Journal of International Law*, vol. 86 (1992), pp. 569–607.

By permitting such discretion to member states, the EC risked rendering its own criteria meaningless.

Four of the six Yugoslav republics—Slovenia, Croatia, Bosnia-Herzegovina, and Macedonia—formally accepted the EC's conditions and applied for recognition. The arbitration commission concluded that Slovenia and Macedonia met the EC's criteria for democracy and the protection of human and minority rights, but raised concerns about protection for minorities in Croatia and Bosnia-Herzegovina.

In two cases, the EC deviated from the commission's recommendations. With the deadline approaching, Croatian president Franjo Tudjman provided the EC with written assurances that his government would respect the rights of the 600,000-strong Serb minority in Croatia. The 12 EC countries, as well as several other European states and Canada, recognized both Slovenia and Croatia on January 15, 1992. Although Macedonia met the EC's criteria on democracy and human rights, Greece objected to use of the name "Macedonia," which also describes a large region of its country, fearing a renewal of border disputes. The EC deferred to the Greek position and denied recognition to Macedonia. Despite repeated assurances from Macedonian leaders that the republic had no territorial designs on Greece, the EC reiterated its position on June 27, 1992—stating unequivocally that Macedonia would not be recognized until it changed its name.[15]

Meanwhile, the EC recommended a referendum on independence for Bosnia-Herzegovina—whose population is 43 percent Slavic Muslim, 31 percent Serb, and 17 percent Croat. In the March referendum, 63 percent of the republic's eligible voters cast ballots, with 99 percent voting in favor of independence. Bosnia's Serb population largely boycotted the referendum. The EC granted recognition to Bosnia-Herzegovina on April 6, 1992.

U.S. policy evolved more slowly. On July 3, 1991, Baker signalled a shift in policy when he indicated that the United States was prepared to accept any new political configuration negotiated by the republics.[16] The United States was not willing to grant separate recognition to any of the republics so long as fighting continued.

U.N. secretary-general Javier Pérez de Cuéllar, Cyrus Vance (Pérez de Cuéllar's envoy to Yugoslavia), and the U.S. government opposed the

---

[15]Radio Free Europe/Radio Liberty, *Daily Report*, no. 121 (June 29, 1992), p. 5.
[16]"War in Yugoslavia Feared by Baker," *New York Times*, July 4, 1991, p. A7.

European Community's moves toward recognition in December 1991 and January 1992, fearing that such action would fatally undermine U.N. and EC peace initiatives. Deputy Secretary of State Lawrence Eagleburger warned EC members on December 13 that early, separate recognition of Croatia and Slovenia would not only damage the prospects for peace but would "almost inevitably lead to greater bloodshed."[17] In a December 14, 1991, letter to German foreign minister Hans-Dietrich Genscher, Pérez de Cuéllar warned that "early, selective and uncoordinated recognition" could block U.N. peace efforts.[18]

The issue was how best to prevent Serbian aggression and to protect the rights of the Serb minorities in Croatia and Bosnia-Herzegovina. A policy of nonrecognition might stay the hand of the Serbians so that their interests and concerns could be addressed through negotiations. There was no evidence, however, that Serbian forces had any intention of not committing aggression if recognition were withheld from Croatia or Bosnia-Herzegovina. Certainly the absence of U.S. recognition made little if any difference. In Bosnia-Herzegovina, for example, the armed conflict commenced weeks before the date of U.S. recognition of the statehood of that republic and months before U.S. recognition of its government. Alternatively, recognition would allow the internationalization of the conflict and the right of other nations to intervene to defend Croatia and Bosnia-Herzegovina from aggression and to protect all minorities, including the Serbs.

After the EC promulgated its recognition guidelines, the United States reiterated four principles guiding its policy toward the republics of Yugoslavia:

a) the United States would accept any outcome chosen peacefully, democratically, and through negotiation;
b) the United States would not recognize changes in internal or external borders achieved through force, intimidation, or threats;
c) the republics must be committed to resolving disputes through peaceful negotiation; and

---

[17]Bush administration official, quoted in "Bonn's Yugoslav Plan Faces More Flak," *New York Times*, December 14, 1991, p. A3.
[18]Quoted in "EC May Soon Recognize Yugoslav States," *L.A. Times*, December 17, 1991, p. A1.

d) the republics must be committed to respecting the human rights of all citizens, including the members of all ethnic groups.[19]

Nowhere in these principles was the prospect for secession acknowledged, even though by December 1991 it could be fairly predicted as a strong possibility. Belgrade could have read these principles as support for the proposition that the republics needed to remain together in a more disciplined, peaceful, and democratic state.

After the European Community and others recognized Slovenia and Croatia, the United States continued to insist on a peace settlement before it would grant recognition. Even if the United States refused to recognize Croatia because of ongoing fighting and insufficient guarantees of minority rights, the rationale for denying recognition to Slovenia was less clear. Slovenia was by then in full control of its own territory and had issued its own currency, its government was democratically chosen in a multiparty election, and its constitution contained full guarantees of human rights. Like the European Community, however, the United States tied the issue of recognition for Slovenia to the issue of recognition for Croatia.

On April 7, 1992, the United States recognized Slovenia, Croatia, and Bosnia-Herzegovina as independent states,[20] but deferred to its Greek ally in the case of Macedonia and had not granted recognition as of mid-1992. The United States waited until August 1992 to recognize and extend full diplomatic ties to the governments of Slovenia, Croatia, and Bosnia-Herzegovina. Despite its recognition of Bosnia-Herzegovina and the pleas of that government for help against the Serbian onslaught, the United States and the European Community were pitifully slow to initiate or support regional or international intervention to respond to aggression, "ethnic cleansing," and other serious violations of international law, including international humanitarian law.

Neither the United States nor the European Community applied its recognition criteria to one of the most troubled and repressed Yugoslav regions—the Serbian province of Kosovo, populated largely by ethnic Albanians. The

---

[19]State Department Regular Briefing, December 5, 1991, Federal News Service Transcript, S-4-6, p. 3.

[20]Statement on United States Recognition of the Former Yugoslav Republics. Reprinted in *Weekly Compilation of Presidential Documents*, vol. 28 (1992), p. 601.

province, like the Serbian province of Vojvodina, was guaranteed autonomy by the 1974 federal Yugoslav constitution. Demonstrations in 1981 by Kosovar Albanians seeking the status of a full republic for Kosovo were met by mass arrests and repression. Serbia has not been able to fully quell the rebellion since and has exacerbated tensions by revoking Kosovo's autonomy.

But Kosovo's claims to autonomy—and, more recently, independence—underscore the complexity of self-determination disputes. Although Albanians make up 90 per cent of the population, Serbs assert a historical claim to Kosovo, which was Serbia's medieval heartland and the site of its defeat by Ottoman Turkey in 1389. Faced with these directly conflicting ethnic and historical claims, the international community has stood back from the dispute, though publicly supporting autonomy for the province. In the meantime, repression continues. Kosovo declared its independence in October 1991, but it was not given the opportunity to apply for EC recognition along with the republics. In May 1992 parliamentary elections declared illegal by Serbia, Kosovar Albanians elected a staunchly pro-independence president and parliament—raising the possibility that without international involvement the Yugoslav conflict would engulf yet another region.[21]

The Iraqi Stalemate

In contrast to the secessionist pressures that ultimately broke up the Soviet Union and Yugoslavia, the situation in Iraq in recent years has involved a very different calculus of self-determination claims. The large Kurdish population of northern Iraq (numbering about 3.5 million) makes up part of the approximately 25 million Kurds who have a long history of similar ethnic and cultural values within the Middle Eastern region of Kurdistan. Kurdistan has never been a sovereign state, but many Iraqi Kurds have long sought, at a minimum, autonomy. Even though the Treaty of Sèvres after World War I held out the promise of autonomy and possible statehood to

---

[21]Strobe Talbott, "The Serbian Death Wish," *Time*, June 1, 1992, p. 74; "Winds of Yugoslavia's War Threaten To Engulf Ethnic Enclave in Serbia," *New York Times*, May 26, 1992, p. A6; "A Different Kind of War in Kosovo: Serbian Repression vs. Quiet Resistance," *New York Times*, June 23, 1992, p. A10.

the many Kurds governed by Turkey, they, along with Kurds in Iran and in the emerging state of Iraq, were denied the opportunity for either.[22]

U.S. involvement with the Iraqi Kurds intensified in the early 1970s. Their leader, Mullah Mustafa Barzani, reached agreement with the Baath regime in 1970 for limited autonomy for the Kurdish people in Iraq. But the agreement was never successfully implemented. Kurdish leaders were encouraged and aided by Iran, Israel, and the United States to destabilize the Baath regime through armed conflict. In 1974, the Iraqi government offered the Kurds a second chance at autonomy by enacting the "Law for Autonomy in the Area of Kurdistan."[23] But it was a one-sided offer that the Kurdish leadership found unacceptable. A devastating civil war followed. Secretary of State Henry Kissinger cut off covert aid to the Kurds, thereby adding to a trail of broken promises long remembered by the Kurdish leadership. Kissinger defended the action as unavoidable in light of congressional opposition to overseas engagements following the Vietnam debacle and other pressures on U.S. foreign policy at that time, including the U.S. relationship with the Shah of Iran. Saddam Hussein negotiated the Algiers Agreement of 1975 with Iran, leading Teheran to terminate aid to the Kurdish forces. The Kurdish revolt was quashed.

The next turning point in U.S. policy toward the Kurds came in August 1988, when hundreds or perhaps thousands of Kurdish villagers were killed through use of chemical weapons by the Iraqi army. This incident took place in the final stages of the Iran-Iraq war and the *Anfal*, a brutal decade-long Iraqi campaign against the Iraqi Kurds that brought an estimated 200,000 deaths, the total destruction of hundreds of Kurdish villages and towns, and the displacement of hundreds of thousands of Kurds. Although the chemical weapon attack was condemned by the United States, the Reagan and Bush administrations blocked persistent congressional efforts to put teeth behind the condemnation with stiff arms and economic sanctions on Iraq. Human rights played the dominant role in the congressional initiative. The policy debate and media coverage of the gas attack as well as the flight of Kurdish refugees into Turkey in 1988 brought the

---

[22]For an excellent summary of the history of the Kurds, see Hurst Hannum, *Autonomy, Sovereignty, and Self-Determination: The Accommodation of Conflicting Rights* (Philadelphia: University of Pennsylvania Press, 1990), pp. 178–202.

[23]See Hannum, pp. 192–93.

plight of the Kurds to national attention. This highly publicized exposure to the Kurdish problem would fortify American and international concern three years later when millions of Kurds fled the Iraqi army after its rout in Kuwait.

Prior to and during the Gulf war of 1991, President Bush encouraged the Iraqi people and military to rebel and overthrow Saddam Hussein's regime.[24] The plea, stated both explicitly and implicitly on several occasions, led many to believe that if the Kurds in northern Iraq and the Shia in southern Iraq revolted, the United States and perhaps some of its coalition allies would provide military assistance to defend the rebellion and achieve the objective of Saddam's downfall. Bush administration officials denied responsibility later, but at the time there was considerable concern that the United States had encouraged rebellion only to abandon the Kurds and Shia during the critical days of the rebellion in March 1991. Although some Kurdish leaders may have been emboldened by Bush's rhetoric, the massive defeat of the Iraqi army in Kuwait and the heavy bombing of Iraq during the Gulf war were probably decisive factors behind the revolt. They offered the Kurds and the Shia (the largest ethnic group of Iraq) an unprecedented—albeit fatal—opportunity to seize the initiative.

In promoting rebellion, the Bush administration never called for the dismemberment of Iraq. In fact, U.S. policy clearly favored maintaining the full territorial integrity and stability of Iraq. The plea from the White House was directed at changing Iraq's national government, potentially encouraging even military officials close to Saddam, provided they steered Iraq toward compliance with the Security Council resolutions and adherence to international law. Saudi Arabia, Turkey, and Syria also strongly opposed the breakup of Iraq. Moreover, neither the Kurds nor the Shia were necessarily seeking independence. While a large faction of the Kurdish population

---

[24]On February 15, 1991, for example, Bush said, "There's another way for the bloodshed to stop, and that is for the Iraqi military and the Iraqi people to take matters into their own hands and force Saddam Hussein, the dictator, to step aside, and then comply with the United Nations resolutions and rejoin the family of peace-loving nations. We have no argument with the people of Iraq. Our differences are with that brutal dictator in Baghdad." Immediately following the conclusion of the ground war, Bush said on March 1, 1991, "In my own view I've always said that the Iraqi people should put [Saddam Hussein] aside, and that would facilitate the resolution of all these problems that exist and certainly would facilitate the acceptance of Iraq back into the family of peace-loving nations." Statements of President George Bush. Reprinted in *Public Papers of the Presidents of the United States: George Bush, 1991*, Book I (Washington, D.C.: U.S. Government Printing Office, 1992), pp. 145 and 198.

advocates secession for Kurdish northern Iraq, the primary objective of the rebellion was to liberate the Kurdish people from Saddam Hussein's rule—whether by establishing an autonomous entity or a newly independent state outside his control or by causing his downfall and establishing a new government in Iraq.

The Kurdish vision for self-determination during the March 1991 rebellion, then, did not focus on a particular form of government or on the dismemberment of Iraq. Nevertheless, it was the beginning of a self-determination struggle. The principle of self-determination and the large-scale uprising it prompted became overwhelmed by the brutal assaults of the Iraqi army on the Kurdish and Shiite populations, which resulted in thousands of refugees streaming north to Turkey, east to Iran, and south to the allied occupied territory of southern Iraq. The United States took no military action in support of the rebellion and, as some (including Bush administration officials) would argue, did not have any U.N. authority to do so.

In mid-April 1991, however, the allies intervened in northern Iraq. They responded to the mass exodus of Kurdish refugees into Turkey and not to any intention on the part of the United States, Britain, and France to defend and guarantee the self-determination of the Kurds. The humanitarian objectives of Operation Provide Comfort were clear.[25] But over time the allied intervention to create a security zone, the U.S. warning to Iraq not to attack the Kurds, and the extensive humanitarian operation enabled the Iraqi Kurds to create a more cohesive political character within a de facto autonomous region of northern Iraq and to pursue options for self-determination.

By May 1992, the Iraqi Kurds found a means to strengthen their commitment to self-determination, albeit again without reaching judgment on the exact territorial status or governmental relationship with Baghdad that they ultimately wanted. Elections were held in Kurdish-controlled northern Iraq on May 19 to establish a new Kurdish national assembly, a new local administration for Kurdish affairs, and a single Kurdish leader. The turnout was impressive. An estimated one million Kurds, or about 88 percent of the eligible electorate, voted. Neither Massoud Barzani (who favors

---

[25]The U.N. Security Council established the humanitarian premise in Resolution 688 of April 5, 1991. For discussion, see David J. Scheffer, "Use of Force After the Cold War: Panama, Iraq, and the New World Order," in Louis Henkin et al., *Right v. Might*, 2d ed. (New York: Council on Foreign Relations, 1991) pp. 144–48.

negotiations with Saddam) nor Jalal Talabani (who favors a complete break with Baghdad) won the necessary majority for the top post and thus faced a runoff later in 1992.

The Iraqi government condemned the elections as illegal. The U.S. State Department reacted cautiously and maintained its support for a unified Iraq:

> We welcome public and private assurances by the Iraqi Kurdish leadership that these elections will deal only with local administrative issues and do not represent a move toward separatism. . . .
>
> The US Government continues to support the sovereignty and territorial integrity of the state of Iraq and to favor replacement of the brutal Saddam Hussein regime with a new government in Baghdad which will fairly represent Iraq's pluralistic society, accept the UN Security Council resolutions, and live at peace with neighboring states. We would like to see all the people of Iraq taking part in a democratic system and enjoying the freedoms which have so long been denied to them by Saddam Hussein. As we have said many times, we do not support the emergence of an independent political entity in northern Iraq.[26]

Thus the U.S. government remained consistent in its desire to replace the Baghdad regime and to maintain the integrity of the state of Iraq.

The practicality of these objectives, however, remained seriously at odds with the situation within Iraq where Saddam's grip on power seemed only to tighten by mid-1992 and where the protection of the Kurdish and Shiite peoples appeared increasingly tied to their control or prospects for control over large regions of Iraq. The U.S. position reflected the concerns of its ally, Turkey, but also the fears of Syria and Iran—three states that opposed the May 1992 elections for fear they would encourage creation of a neighboring Iraqi Kurdish state and stir up the secessionist aspirations of Kurds within their own states.[27]

---

[26]Statement of May 15, 1992. Reprinted in *U.S. Department of State Dispatch*, vol. 3 (1992), p. 385.

[27]"Iraqi Kurds' Parliament Raises Neighbors' Fears of Kurdish State," *Washington Post*, June 28, 1992, p. A29.

By July 1992, however, senior officials in Kuwait and Saudi Arabia started to consider the merits of a partitioned Iraq while Washington strengthened its ties to Iraqi opposition groups. In the Gulf, Kuwait and Saudi officials argued "privately and sometimes publicly that the partition of Iraq into several entities—Shiites in the south, Kurds in the north and Sunnis in the center—may be the key to neutralizing a country whose population is increasingly viewed by oil-rich gulf Arab states as inherently aggressive."[28]

In Washington, a group of top Iraqi opposition leaders—including Kurdish, Shiite, and Sunni figures—met with Secretary of State James Baker for the first time. The Iraqis represented the Iraqi National Congress, a body of Iraqi opposition groups created in Vienna in June 1992 that agreed upon a right of self-determination for the Kurds.[29] They sought U.S. recognition for an anti-Saddam government-in-exile that might be established in northern Iraq. While Baker refused to go that far, the Iraqis' visit elevated their relationship with the United States. Baker issued a statement that urged them to continue to unify in order to create "a democratic, pluralistic government which lives in peace with its neighbors and cares for its people." The United States was still opting for a stable, democratic, whole Iraq but one re-created by a unified coalition of opposition groups. Baker went on to promise that the United States "will continue to stand firmly in support of the brave Iraqis who oppose Saddam's tyranny."[30]

Whether Baker's promise meant that the United States would use military force to support another rebellion or to defend the Kurds or the Shia from Saddam's internal aggression remained an open question.[31] One answer would be to firmly commit to the protection of the Kurds with the guarantee of allied military intervention (in addition to air support) in response to an Iraqi army move into northern Iraq, and to the defense of the Shia by creating a "humanitarian zone" in southern Iraq that also would benefit from the

---

[28]"Gulf Arabs Thinking of a Divided Iraq," *New York Times*, August 2, 1992, p. 12. However, the Iraqi Shia may seek a far greater role in the Iraqi government rather than secession. See "Iraqi Shiites Say Goal is Power Sharing, Not Independence," *Washington Post*, August 23, 1992, p. A19.

[29]"An Opportunity to Show Our Resolve," *Washington Times*, July 3, 1992, p. F4.

[30]"Baker Meets Iraqi Opposition; U.S. to Approach U.N. on Force," *Washington Post*, July 30, 1992, p. A20.

[31]National Security Adviser Brent Scowcroft reportedly told the opposition leaders, "We won't let you down." See Jim Hoagland, " 'We Won't Let You Down'," *Washington Post*, August 4, 1992, p. A19.

guarantee of allied military intervention if that were to prove necessary.[32] If this were done, a momentum might develop whereby distinct autonomy or independence for the Kurdish north and the Shiite south would become more palatable to the U.S. government and Iraq's neighbors. But even by mid-1992, the impression remained that the U.S. government simply had not thought through the issue of the integrity of Iraq and whether the creation of autonomous regions, or several new states, or even a radically reconstituted central government (perhaps beginning as a "government-in-exile"), would better serve long-range U.S. interests in the region.

---

[32]"U.S. Begins Planning for Possible Clash with Iraq," *Los Angeles Times*, July 29, 1992, p. 1.

Chapter Three

A MODERN UNDERSTANDING OF SELF-DETERMINATION

The self-determination claims threatening the new world order demand a new approach from the United States and the world community. There is a clear need to recognize the changing political circumstances in the world and the variety of movements that raise the banner of self-determination. In this chapter, we set the stage for presenting a new approach by examining the weaknesses of the United States' and international community's handling of self-determination disputes and introducing new categories of self-determination.

Weaknesses in the Current Approach

A major innovation in the world community's response to the breakup of the Soviet Union and of Yugoslavia was the development of criteria for support or recognition that focus on the relationship between the government and its people. We strongly support this change in approach. However, there have been significant deficiencies both in how the United States and the international community have approached self-determination claims in the post–Cold War era and in the specific criteria they have laid out. These deficiencies include:

Timing of the Response. The United States and the international community have responded only grudgingly to self-determination claims in the post–Cold War era. In Yugoslavia, the signs of a breakup existed long before Slovenia and Croatia declared independence in June 1991. Recognition criteria for the republics of the Soviet Union were promulgated only after the country's breakup became inevitable. For a long time the U.S. government and other governments simply repeated their support for the unity of the state, without pressing for the reforms that might have made that possible.

Eurocentric Standards. The United States and the European Community each promulgated standards that were tailor-made for the successor states of either the Soviet Union or Yugoslavia. No coordinated, systematic effort was undertaken to develop standards that had a more universal relevance, including application to the self-determination movements active within the Yugoslav and Soviet successor states.

Inconsistent Application of Standards. There will be times when one standard must be balanced against another or against an overriding national interest. But the principle of self-determination should not be held hostage to selective applications of standards. The United States and the European Community, for example, have not consistently applied their criteria for recognition among the Soviet and Yugoslav successor states pledging adherence to those criteria. There is a weakness in the "standards" themselves if they are not consistently applied.

Lack of Enforcement. It is not surprising that the criteria laid out to date include no enforcement mechanism. A government is recognized once it asserts that it accepts the criteria and convinces observers that those criteria are being adhered to at the moment. Two days, two months, or two years later it may deviate from the criteria, leaving the international community with no clear authority to act.

New Categories of Self-Determination

As self-determination movements proliferate, it is more difficult for states to respond effectively, largely because their policies amount to blanket rejections of self-determination claims. Yet the reality of the post–Cold War era is that the challenges of self-determination movements are not likely to abate in the near future. Self-determination movements are decidedly not all alike or even similar to each other.

As a first step toward a modern approach, governments must adopt a broader and less alarmist view of self-determination. The full exercise of self-determination need not result in the outcome predicted by those who would discredit the principle—independent statehood for every single ethnic group. Rather, the full exercise of self-determination can lead to a number of outcomes, ranging from minority-rights protections, to cultural or political autonomy, to independent statehood. The principle of self-determination is best viewed as entitling a people to choose its political allegiance, to influence the political order under which it lives, and to preserve its cultural, ethnic, historical, or territorial identity. Often, although not always, these objectives can be achieved with less than full independence.

This broader view of self-determination, however, does not resolve the critical question of what constitutes a "people" for the purposes of self-determination. Governments often have sought to narrow the definition of "peoples" in order to limit the number of groups entitled to exercise a self-determination claim. Groups making such claims, meanwhile, have pressed for a broader application of the term. These different approaches are reflected in contemporary disputes. For example, indigenous communities attached particular importance to the 1989 revision of the International Labour Organisation's convention on the protection of indigenous rights, in which the language referring to indigenous communities changed from "populations" to "peoples."[1] Similarly, a number of states sought to keep indigenous communities out of the working group sessions of the 1992 U.N. Conference on Environment and Development by seeking a qualification of the term "peoples."[2]

In defining "peoples" for the purpose of weighing their claims to self-determination, we favor the approach of a number of scholars.[3] In identifying a "unit" that may have a claim to self-determination, the United States and the international community should not focus on a single criterion, such as distinct ethnicity, but should weigh both objective and subjective factors. Objectively, whether a group is a "people" for the purposes of self-determination depends on the extent to which the group making a claim

---

[1]Indigenous and Tribal Populations Convention, 1957 (No. 107); Indigenous and Tribal Peoples Convention, 1989 (No. 169).

[2]Seminar on "Evolving Boundaries of Self-Determination," Yale Law School, New Haven, Connecticut, April 11, 1992.

[3]Lung-Chu Chen, "Self-Determination and World Public Order," *Notre Dame Law Review*, vol. 66 (1991), p. 1290; Ved P. Nanda, "Self-Determination Under International Law: Validity of Claims to Secede," *Case Western Reserve Journal of International Law*, vol. 13 (1981), pp. 275–76; Lee C. Buchheit, *Secession: The Legitimacy of Self-Determination* (New Haven: Yale University Press, 1978), pp. 9–11.

shares ethnic, linguistic, religious, or cultural bonds, although the absence or weakness of one of these bonds need not invalidate a claim. The subjective standard should weigh the extent to which members within the group perceive the group's identity as distinct from the identities of other groups.

The second step in developing a new approach to handling self-determination claims is to recognize that not all self-determination claims are alike. Throughout the twentieth century, the practice of most scholars has been to distinguish only between "external" and "internal" claims—that is, between claims to freedom from alien domination and claims to a new governing regime within an existing territory. This distinction fails to capture the wider range of challenges and dilemmas that self-determination movements now present to the international community. The international community must respond to this greater complexity not by simply resisting self-determination claims, but by adopting a framework for distinguishing among them and assessing their legitimacy.

As a step toward this goal, we abandon the conventional terminology of "external" and "internal" self-determination and introduce descriptive terminology appropriate for the post-Cold War world. The terms "external" and "internal" not only are inadequate to deal with the complexities of the challenges posed by self-determination movements, they can also cause considerable confusion. The potential difficulty is described by Lee Buchheit:

> The problem of a segment of a State wishing to disassociate itself from the unified country falls neatly into an interstice between internal and external self-determination. The seceding province obviously wishes to readjust its political status vis-à-vis the remaining State (which seems an aspect of internal self-determination); yet by proclaiming itself an independent entity it may apparently resist any attempt at forced reunification under the principle of external self-determination (the parent State having become an "outside party").[4]

The categories of self-determination claims proposed here merely distinguish among types of claims; they are not a judgment of legitimacy in principle or under international law.

---

[4]Buchheit, pp. 15–16.

Anti-Colonial Self-Determination. A claim to "anti-colonial" self-determination refers to a territorial population under colonial rule or alien domination that seeks complete freedom or more political power. This differs from the conventional term, "external self-determination," to avoid confusion with separatist movements within the boundaries of existing states that seek to redefine their relationship with the central government as an "external" relationship. The phenomenon of anti-colonial self-determination claims is largely historical, although the potential for such claims may exist in Puerto Rico, New Caledonia, the Falkland Islands, Gibraltar, and elsewhere.

There may be certain sub-state self-determination claims (defined below) that also have an anti-colonial character. Take, for example, the Palestinian and, until recently, the Estonian and Ukrainian movements. If the incorporation of an area was the result of forceful expansion, whether as an act of aggression or of self-defense, the question becomes whether the conquering government made a reasonable effort to integrate the population of the area into a representative government under which, for a period at least, the politically active population felt adequately represented. By these criteria, the Estonian and Palestinian movements might be anti-colonial, because of the failure to fully integrate the population, whereas the Ukrainian movement would be more questionable and hence regarded more as an example of sub-state self-determination.

Sub-State Self-Determination. "Sub-state" self-determination describes the attempt of a group within an existing state to break off and form a new state or to achieve a greater degree of political or cultural autonomy within the existing state.[5] Sub-state self-determination movements may be based on ethnic, geographic, historical, or economic factors. They include only claims by groups concentrated in a particular geographic area; claims of dispersed peoples are treated in a separate category. Examples of sub-state self-determination movements include ethnic claims such as those of Tibet or of the Sikh community in Punjab; economic claims such as that of Siberia; or geographic and historical claims such as that of the independence

---

[5]We avoid using more common terms such as "secessionist" or "separatist" self-determination, to emphasize that a sub-state movement may not seek full independence and that self-determination claims can often be resolved with steps short of full independence. There will be circumstances, discussed later in this book, when these terms will be applicable.

movement on Taiwan. Most movements are likely to combine several of these factors.

Sub-state claims often have been reasonably met by federalism. Francophone movements in Canada, Tamil movements in India, and Ibo movements in Nigeria have been contained—albeit with occasional eruptions—within federal structural bargains. For many years, the same could have been said for Tamil claims in Sri Lanka or Albanian claims in the Serbian province of Kosovo in Yugoslavia. Once the federal bargains were broken by Prime Minister S. W. R. D. Bandaranaike in the mid-1950s in the case of Sri Lanka and, more recently, by Serbian president Slobodan Milošević in the case of Yugoslavia, the sub-state claims focused on demands for full independence.

Trans-State Self-Determination. A self-determination claim involving the concentrated grouping of a people in more than one existing state may be called a "trans-state" claim.[6] An ethnic group may cut across existing international boundaries, as do the Kurds and the Basques. A group may seek to break away from one existing state and accede to another state; examples include Armenians in Nagorno-Karabakh seeking to become part of Armenia, majority ethnic Romanians in Moldova seeking ties to Romania, some movements in Kashmir favoring union with Pakistan, or ethnic Russians in the Crimea seeking to secede from Ukraine and join Russia.

Alternatively, a group pleading a trans-state claim may seek to establish an independent, unitary state carved out of two or more existing states. An independent Kurdistan or Kashmir would represent this possibility. Trans-state claims can pose particularly difficult questions—as in the case of the Kurds, whose leaders in Turkey, Iraq, Syria, and the Caucasus may have different ideas about the future of the Kurdish movement.

Irredentist claims add a potentially volatile element to trans-state self-determination. Russia's interest in Russian populations now located in numerous Soviet successor states illustrates the possibility of irredentist claims leading to conflict.

Self-Determination of Dispersed Peoples. The claims of peoples dispersed throughout one or more states are proposed as a separate category to

---

[6]We purposely do not employ the term "transnational." We seek to avoid the confusion that can stem from the use of "nation" to designate an ethnic and cultural community and the use of "nation" to designate a state.

distinguish them from claims involving a geographically concentrated people. Situations involving ethnically or culturally distinct peoples intermixed throughout the same territory are potentially more volatile, as is illustrated by the conflict in Bosnia-Herzegovina. Implementing local self-government or autonomy arrangements where different peoples are dispersed can be far more difficult than in territories with geographically concentrated groups.

Sometimes it is not even clear whether the people in fact are dispersed or concentrated. At the time of India's decolonization, the dispute between the Indian National movement and the Muslim movement was over whether Muslims were dispersed or concentrated. The British decided in favor of the Muslim claim—that Muslims were concentrated—and created a separate Pakistan. Similarly, a dispersed people may be seeking concentration and hence a claim to independent statehood. The critical response to self-determination claims of dispersed peoples is the development of truly representative and preferably democratic government, where the interests of the dispersed minority can be adequately and fairly addressed. A focus on democracy and protection of non-territorial minority rights (as well as each individual's human rights) thus might be the most effective way of addressing the self-determination claims of dispersed peoples.

Indigenous Self-Determination. The claims of indigenous communities—that is, groups characterized by a distinct ethnicity and long historical continuity with a pre-colonial or pre-invasion society—pose a special challenge. Indigenous communities may inhabit a geographically concentrated area, cut across international boundaries, or be dispersed throughout an area, but their claims are regarded here as a distinct category because handling them often requires greater sensitivity to political culture and traditions. Demands of indigenous groups range from independent statehood to meaningful forms of autonomy to control of land or resources. Contemporary examples of indigenous self-determination claims are those of indigenous communities in Guatemala and Nicaragua, Native Americans, the aboriginal peoples of Australia, and various groups in Canada, including the Cree Indians of northern Quebec (who seek to remain in federation with Canada and would be denied that right by Quebec's secession from Canada).[7]

---

[7]A discussion of proposed self-government for Canada's indigenous peoples appears in "Canada Pact Aims to Preserve Unity," *New York Times*, August 23, 1992, p. 15.

Representative Self-Determination. A claim to "representative" self-determination results when the population of an existing state seeks to change its political structure in favor of a more representative (and preferably democratic) structure. By using the term "representative," we do not mean to deny to other types of self-determination claims the goal of more representation, or self-government, of the people involved. In fact, a goal of better representation can underpin self-determination claims of all types. Rather, we use "representative" here, for lack of a more descriptive term, to describe what is conventionally labelled with the potentially confusing term "internal self-determination." Contemporary examples of states whose populations are seeking to change their political structure include South Africa, Haiti, and Myanmar (formerly Burma). The catalyst for change need not be restricted to a popular protest; a change in national governance could occur through a negotiated solution, as in Cambodia. While democracy is not necessarily the goal of some representative self-determination movements, many regard a democratic government for the country as a whole to be the most effective and realistic way to protect minority rights. Some Kurdish leaders, for example, have advocated democracy for Iraq rather than secession for the Kurdish people.

These categories do not pretend to be comprehensive. Moreover, a particular self-determination movement may fit in more than one category. Still, we believe that a framework that recognizes the complex nature of contemporary self-determination demands and distinguishes among them in the manner presented here will be helpful in determining how to think about a specific situation and to craft an appropriate resolution.

Chapter Four

DEVELOPMENTS IN INTERNATIONAL LAW

e have shown how international law during the Cold War confined the principle of self-determination to anti-colonial movements, and how that principle has yet to embrace as binding law other forms of self-determination. A group seeking to secede from an existing state may not find an enforceable right in international law to support the breakup of the state.[1] However, international law is beginning to evolve in the post–Cold War period toward a more expansive view of issues that bear directly upon the demands for self-determination. Governments, particularly in Europe and North America, are broadening their own understanding of international law on self-determination, human rights, and the use of force.

We review in this chapter three aspects of international law that are directly relevant to the development of a new approach by the United States and the world community toward self-determination claims. Developments in the protection of minority rights, the promotion of democracy, and the law of recognition point, together with new perspectives on the law of self-determination itself, toward the evolution of a new regime of international law to govern self-determination claims. As we have emphasized, for both domestic and international reasons, concerned governments will need to work toward general principles that will be acceptable to the international community.

---

[1]See pp. 16–25.

Protection of Minority Rights

International law is evolving to provide greater protection for minority rights, in part because such protection has the potential to prevent the dismemberment of a multiethnic state. But during the Cold War, the concept of minority rights was narrowly construed and rarely applied.

As with many other aspects of international law much debate concerns definitions: What is a minority, the type of group that might strive for secession or claim additional protection under a state's laws? International lawyers have never agreed on a universal definition. Historically, minorities were generally viewed as "a numerically smaller, non-dominant group distinguished by shared ethnic, racial, religious, or linguistic attributes."[2] This historical definition, however, describes only part of the modern view of minority groups. The existence of a minority meriting protection requires not only shared attributes, but also the "imagination" of a community based on those attributes. This subjective factor includes how the members of a group perceive the group's identity as distinct from the identity of other groups.

The protection of minority rights can be discovered in a series of bilateral European treaties, dating back to 1606, that gave limited recognition to a minority's freedom to practice a different religion within the state.[3] By the nineteenth century, the protection of minorities had broadened to include guarantees of civil and political rights as well as religious freedom.[4] In 1815, the Congress of Vienna included factors of ethnicity and language in addressing the governance of certain minorities.[5] A legal regime for the

---

[2]Hurst Hannum, *Autonomy Sovereignty, and Self-Determination: The Accommodation of Conflicting Rights* (Philadelphia: University of Pennsylvania Press, 1990), p. 50.

[3]Stephen Ryan, *Ethnic Conflict and International Relations* (Brookfield, Vermont: Dartmouth, 1990), p. 152; Hannum, pp. 50–51.

[4]Frank Koszorus, Jr., "The Forgotten Legacy of the League of Nations Minority Protection System" in *Essays on World War I: Total War and Peacemaking, A Case Study on Trianon*, vol. 6 of *War and Society in East Central Europe*, ed. Béla K. Király, Peter Pastor, and Ivan Sanders (New York: Brooklyn College Press, 1982), p. 548.

[5]Hannum, p. 51. Article I of the General Treaty, for example, protected the Polish minorities in Russia, Austria, and Prussia by calling for "Representation and National Institutions, regulated according to the degree of political consideration, that each of the Governments to which they belong shall judge expedient and proper to grant them." Michael Hurst, ed., *Key Treaties of the Great Powers*, vol. 1, *1814–1870* (New York: St. Martin's Press, 1972), p. 45.

protection of minority rights did not evolve, however, until the end of World War I and the creation of the League of Nations. Even then, there was no international law to protect minority rights. Rather, the League entered into a series of treaties with some newly-created and some reconfigured European states to ensure the protection of the rights of certain minority groups in the Europe of the 1920s.

Among the rights protected under the League's minority treaties were the right to freedom from discrimination, regardless of race, language, or religion; the right to use one's own language in private and public forums; and the right to citizenship. The treaties gave minorities the right to establish and control their own charitable, religious, social, and educational institutions. They also placed upon states an obligation to give equitable funding to minority schools, with instruction at the primary level available in the language of the minority.[6]

The hope was that if the League could guarantee minority groups these rights, the pressures for separate statehood could be offset. In some respects, the minority treaties of the League era were aimed at quieting ethnic discord. In exchange for League supervision of minorities, the participating states protected their own sovereignty and territorial integrity. Likewise, the minorities were, to some extent, protected from the nationalistic zeal of their central governments.

Under the minority treaties, an individual of a protected minority group could petition the League's secretariat with a grievance. Five review procedures within the League bureaucracy automatically followed, culminating in optional consideration of the grievance in a formal session of the League membership. But the League had no enforcement powers. It only had the power to persuade a recalcitrant government to protect the interests of its minority population; more often than not, it favored the government's position.[7]

Despite the ultimate failure of the League's minority protection regime and of the League itself, the strengths and weaknesses of that regime are instructive in the post–Cold War period. The most obvious weakness was

---

[6]Hannum, pp. 52–53; Koszorus, pp. 550–51. See also the documents on minority rights of the League of Nations and the United Nations collected in Louis B. Sohn and Thomas Buergenthal, eds., *International Protection of Human Rights* (Indianapolis: Bobbs-Merrill, 1973), pp. 213–335.

[7]Ryan, pp. 153–55; Hannum, p. 54.

that the minority treaties were imposed only on a handful of small defeated states and several new states. Germany was not bound by the system. Nor were the Great Powers. But for the first time, minority rights were supervised by an international body pursuant to treaty obligations, marking a significant advance in the concept of minority rights protection.

However, capitalizing upon the absence of effective protection for the rights of German-speaking individuals in Czechoslovakia, Hitler undermined the concept of the right of the international community to protect minorities when he used the presence of German-speaking minorities in Czechoslovakia and elsewhere as pretexts to seize the territory of other European states.

After World War II, the protection of minorities receded as both a political concern and a legal right. There is no mention of minority rights in the U.N. Charter (1945) or the Universal Declaration of Human Rights (1948). The notable exception immediately after the war was the Genocide Convention (1948), which indirectly refers to minority groups in its formulation of a right of existence for human groups. Article 2 of the Convention sets out numerous acts that, when committed "with intent to destroy, in whole or in part, a national, ethnical, racial or religious group," amount to genocide. Minority groups are thus entitled to protection from the various acts of genocide listed in Article 2.[8]

In large part because of the influence of the United States and Eleanor Roosevelt, who was the first U.S. representative on the U.N. Human Rights Commission, the protection of *individual* human rights became the dominant human rights concern. The protection of the individual encouraged the view that the way to manage minority groups was to assimilate them within an existing state, rather than cater to their group identities or cultivate any possible interest in self-determination. With a few exceptions, minority rights were essentially buried as an international legal concern.[9]

Minority rights reappeared in Article 27 of the 1966 International Covenant on Civil and Political Rights, which states:

> In those States in which ethnic, religious or linguistic minorities exist, persons belonging to such minorities shall not be denied the

---

[8]Patrick Thornberry, *Minorities and Human Rights Law* (London: Minority Rights Group, 1991), p. 13.

[9]Hannum, pp. 58–59. See, however, the various post-war treaties cited in Sohn and Buergenthal, pp. 306–11.

right, in community with the other members of their group, to enjoy their own culture, to profess and practise their own religion, or to use their own language.

The rights (culture, religion, language) protected, however, for many years were viewed as limited in scope and lacking sufficient definition. Further, the beneficiary is the individual member of the minority group and not the group as a whole.[10] This interpretation prevails as the dominant view.

In the aftermath of the Cold War, minority rights in a collective sense have found their expression again in several important documents, some still awaiting completion. A working group of the U.N. Sub-Commission on Prevention of Discrimination and Protection of Minorities has prepared a draft Declaration on the Rights of Minorities, completing a second reading of the draft in December of 1991. It is not a manifesto for self-determination; in its preamble it affirms protection of minority rights as a contribution "to the political and social stability of States in which [the ethnic, religious, or linguistic group lives]." It describes "the constant promotion and realization of the rights of persons belonging to national or ethnic, religious and linguistic minorities" in the context of "the development of society as a whole and within a democratic framework based on the rule of law." The draft Declaration's operative provisions reinforce the rights of minorities within states and prohibit any construction of the document's provisions to permit activity "contrary to the purposes and principles of the United Nations, including sovereign equality, territorial integrity and political independence of States."[11]

The Conference on Security and Cooperation in Europe (CSCE) has taken a renewed interest in minority rights, particularly at its Conference on the Human Dimension, held in June 1990 in Copenhagen. The Copenhagen Document includes an entire section on the rights of national minorities and strongly affirms linguistic freedom for minorities as well as the right of

---

[10]Louis B. Sohn, "The Rights of Minorities," in *The International Bill of Rights: The Covenant on Civil and Political Rights*, ed. Louis Henkin (New York: Columbia University Press, 1981), pp. 270–74 and 282–87.

[11]U.N. Commission on Human Rights, *Report of the Working Group on the Rights of Persons Belonging to National, Ethnic, Religious and Linguistic Minorities*, December 16, 1991, Annex I, "Draft Declaration on the Rights of Persons Belonging to National or Ethnic, Religious and Linguistic Minorities" (New York: United Nations, 1992), Article 8.4.

national minorities to establish and maintain their own educational institutions. It notes the efforts by states to establish "appropriate local or autonomous administrations" for minority groups.[12] Though weakly stated, this provision of the Copenhagen Document suggests that democracy and individual human rights guarantees alone may not adequately protect minorities—that it may be necessary to devolve to a minority group as a whole certain political functions and powers (presumably within a portion of the territory of the state) in order to protect not only minority rights but also the territorial integrity of the state.

The Charter of Paris for a New Europe, signed by CSCE heads of state and government on November 21, 1990, echoes the Copenhagen Document's concern for minority rights, when it states: "We affirm that the ethnic, cultural, linguistic and religious identity of national minorities will be protected and that persons belonging to national minorities have the right freely to express, preserve and develop that identity without any discrimination and in full equality before the law."[13]

The Report of the Geneva CSCE Meeting of Experts on National Minorities, adopted July 19, 1991, goes further in fusing protection of minority rights with democratic systems and the rule of law:

> Human rights and fundamental freedoms are the basis for the protection and promotion of rights of persons belonging to national minorities. . . . Questions relating to national minorities can only be satisfactorily resolved in a democratic political framework based on the rule of law, with a functioning independent judiciary. This framework guarantees full respect for human rights and fundamental freedoms, equal rights and status for all citizens, including persons belonging to national minorities, the free expression of all their legitimate interests and aspirations, political pluralism, social tolerance and the implementation of legal rules that place effective restraints on the abuse of government power.

---

[12]See Conference on Security and Cooperation in Europe, "Document of the Copenhagen Meeting of the Conference on the Human Dimension of the CSCE," June 29, 1990. Reprinted in *International Legal Materials*, vol. 29 (September 1990), pp.1318–1320.

[13]Conference on Security and Cooperation in Europe, "Charter of Paris for a New Europe," November 21, 1990. Reprinted in *International Legal Materials*, vol. 30 (January 1991), p. 195.

> Issues concerning national minorities, as well as compliance with international obligations and commitments concerning the rights of persons belonging to them, are matters of legitimate international concern and consequently do not constitute exclusively an internal affair of the respective State.[14]

The Report describes positive results in democratic systems as including "local and autonomous administration, as well as autonomy on a territorial basis, including the existence of consultative, legislative and executive bodies chosen through free and periodic elections," and other forms of decentralized government for national minorities.[15]

A more extreme endorsement of minority rights was, as of summer 1992, being considered by the Council of Europe. The European Commission for Democracy through Law, a consultative body of the Council of Europe on matters of constitutional law, prepared a draft "European Convention for the Protection of Minorities" in Venice in early 1991 that will be submitted to members of the Council for ratification.[16] The draft Venice Convention essentially would require blanket protection for minorities, including protection "against any activity capable of threatening their existence" (Article 3(1)), "the right to freely preserve, express and develop their cultural identity in all its aspects, free of any attempts at assimilation against their will" (Article 6(1)), schooling in the minority's mother tongue (Article 9), effective remedies before national authorities for violations of minority rights (Article 11), and the "effective participation of minorities in public affairs" (Article 14(1)). One of the most controversial provisions (Article 13) would require that states "refrain from pursuing or encouraging policies aimed at the assimilation of minorities or aimed at intentionally modifying the proportions of the population in the regions inhabited by minorities." This would appear to be an anti-integration stance, even when the government's efforts to promote integration are non-coercive.

---

[14]Conference on Security and Cooperation in Europe, "Report of the CSCE Meeting of Experts on National Minorities," July 1–19, 1991. Reprinted in *International Legal Materials*, vol. 30 (November 1991), pp. 1692–1702.

[15]CSCE, "National Minorities," p. 1698.

[16]Council of Europe, European Commission for Democracy through Law, "Proposal for a European Convention for the Protection of Minorities," Strasbourg, March 4, 1991.

The traditional rights of minorities—religion, language, and culture—are embodied in international law, particularly when expressed in terms of the individual belonging to a minority. Beyond that, despite the advances in the documents just described, governments remain reluctant to obligate themselves to protect group rights that they fear may lead to secessionist pressures. Governments are even less willing to grant minority groups the political freedom to wage a campaign for secession that could ultimately lead to the disaggregation of the country. The real mistake occurs when a government is so fearful of self-determination—even when it is not aimed at secession—that it denies minority groups the protection of their traditional rights.[17] Such negativist actions can easily trigger minority discontent and upheaval and create the surge toward self-determination that the government so fears.

The reassertion of the protection of minority rights, particularly by the CSCE and the Council of Europe, points the way toward international or regional involvement in a self-determination dispute where a minority's rights are being violated. The goal of that involvement must initially be to press a government to see that its self-interest lies in accommodating the interests of a minority group, rather than in triggering more extreme self-determination claims—even secessionist demands—by alienating it. Only if such efforts fail is it necessary to consider whether the protection of minority rights justifies support for the creation of a new state.

An "Entitlement" to Democratic Government

In recent years the interrelationship between human rights and democracy has become so pronounced that some scholars now speak of an "entitlement" to democracy as an emerging principle of international law that will create a right or even an obligation for the international community to act to protect or promote democracy.[18] The United States has a strong

---

[17]Hurst Hannum, "Contemporary Developments in the International Protection of the Rights of Minorities," *Notre Dame Law Review*, vol. 66 (1991), p. 1447.

[18]See Thomas M. Franck, "The Emerging Right to Democratic Governance," *American Journal of International Law*, vol. 86 (1992), pp. 46–91. For differing views on this theory, see "National Sovereignty Revisited: Perspectives on the Emerging Norm of Democracy in International Law," *Proceedings of the 86th Annual Meeting of the American Society of International Law* (Washington, D.C.: American Society of International Law, forthcoming 1992).

interest in promoting this trend in part because it gives the United States and other democratic governments a means to press for a form of government in a new state that will grant democratic rights to its people. The granting of such rights should help in many cases to resolve self-determination claims and to prevent secession and violence.

The major democracies and multilateral institutions are extending, consolidating, and defending democratic processes and principles throughout much of the world. As a result, governments of existing and newly emerging states are beginning to see democracy as their gateway to legitimacy. The change is profound, for in the past people could not look to international law to legitimate or protect a "right" to democratic governance.

The foreign policies of major Western democracies now include, or are beginning to include, democratization as a key criterion for the type of relationship that can be built with newly emerging states as well as existing non-democratic states. The United States, Germany, and the United Kingdom are leaders in this area. Beyond the foreign policies of individual governments, however, the emerging commitment to democracy has become an important principle in the work of the Conference on Security and Cooperation in Europe, the Organization of American States, and the United Nations. These bodies are now deeply involved in election and human rights monitoring, in helping to create governments dedicated to democracy, and in helping to institutionalize, consolidate, and preserve democratic government. As the United Nations and regional organizations become more deeply involved in the resolution of armed conflicts, particularly those caused by the pressures of self-determination, both human rights and democratic standards of conduct will become key elements in long-term strategies designed to prevent further outbreaks of violence and to build legitimate structures of government and, if necessary, new states.

The advocacy of democratic governance as an emerging principle of international law has influenced and will continue to influence both the character of self-determination movements and the international community's response to them. On the other hand, Western-style democracy has not taken hold in much of Asia and Africa, and governments and scholars there vigorously contest any presumption of democracy as a legal entitlement.

A brief review of several CSCE documents reveals the extent to which democratic principles are being embodied in politically binding regional and international instruments. In the Copenhagen Document of June 1990, the

CSCE calls democracy and the rule of law "essential for ensuring respect for all human rights and fundamental freedoms" and pledges "to build democratic societies based on free elections and the rule of law."[19] As one scholar has observed, with the Copenhagen Document the CSCE "proclaimed a new pan-European public order, a public order based on democratic pluralism. This democratic public order rejects political systems that are incompatible with representative democracies with respect for fundamental human rights and with the rule of law."[20]

The CSCE's commitment to democracy and human rights was reaffirmed five months later, when CSCE heads of government signed the Charter of Paris for a New Europe. The charter calls human rights and fundamental freedoms the "birthright of all human beings" and their protection and promotion "the first responsibility of government." It commits CSCE states to "co-operate and support each other with the aim of making democratic gains irreversible."[21]

Meeting in Moscow in 1991, representatives of the CSCE created more assertive, collective means to protect human rights within CSCE states and to promote democratic principles. The Moscow Document pledges to condemn the overthrow or attempted overthrow of a democratically elected government and to "support vigorously . . . the legitimate organs of that State upholding human rights, democracy and the rule of law." The Document acknowledges "the need to make further peaceful efforts concerning human rights, democracy and the rule of law within the context of security and co-operation in Europe, individually and collectively, to make democratic advances irreversible."[22]

Thus, the legal principle of non-interference in the internal affairs of states[23] is beginning to be eclipsed in Europe by a commitment to promote democratic pluralism, human rights, and fundamental freedms. Whether

---

[19]CSCE, "Document of the Copenhagen Meeting," p. 1307.

[20]Thomas Buergenthal, "Democratization and Europe's New Public Order," in *CSCE and the New Blueprint for Europe*, ed. Marilyn Wyatt (Washington, D.C.: Georgetown University Institute for the Study of Diplomacy, 1991), p. 53.

[21]CSCE, "Charter of Paris," p. 194.

[22]Conference on Security and Cooperation in Europe, "Document of the Moscow Meeting of the Conference on the Human Dimension of the CSCE," October 3, 1991. Reprinted in *International Legal Materials*, vol. 30 (November 1991), p. 1677.

[23]U.N. Charter, Article 2(7).

that commitment would include support for a separatist movement embracing those principles remains questionable, although the CSCE has not resisted the emergence of new states in Europe and Central Asia. In fact, the membership of the CSCE has grown dramatically as the organization has embraced the new states arising out of the breakup of the Soviet Union and of Yugoslavia.

Similar but less ambitious developments are unfolding in the Western Hemisphere. According to the charter of the Organization of American States, one of the organization's essential purposes is "to promote and consolidate representative democracy."[24] In June 1991, the OAS General Assembly adopted a resolution establishing the capacity to respond rapidly to any "sudden or irregular interruption of the democratic political institutional process of the legitimate exercise of power by the democratically elected government in any of the Organization's member states."[25] When Haitian president Jean-Bertrand Aristide was overthrown in a September 1991 military coup, the OAS Permanent Council adopted a resolution condemning the coup and calling for the restoration of the president's constitutional authority.[26] In April 1992, when Peruvian president Alberto Fujimori suspended the constitution, dissolved the congress and the judiciary, and temporarily imposed press censorship, an emergency meeting of OAS foreign ministers voted 32–0 to "strongly deplore" the actions, calling for an immediate return to constitutional government.[27]

Electoral democracy has been endorsed by the United Nations. The U.N. General Assembly adopted two resolutions in 1991 stressing the importance of "periodic and genuine elections" as a "necessary and indispensable element" in the enjoyment of human rights. It also has created administrative means to help organize elections.[28]

As governments and multilateral institutions embrace and promote democracy, the international community is showing a greater willingness to help resolve internal disputes of states, in some cases even implicitly or

---

[24]OAS Charter, Article 2(b).

[25]OAS G.A. Res. 1080, June 5, 1991, unanimous.

[26]OAS Permanent Council Res. 567, September 30, 1991, unanimous. See, further, OAS Ministers of Foreign Affairs Resolutions 1/91 (October 3, 1991), 2/91 (October 8, 1991), and 3/92 (May 17, 1992).

[27]"OAS Vote Urges Peru to Restore Constitution," *Washington Post*, April 14, 1992, p. A17.

[28]U.N.G.A. Res. 45/150 (XLV), February 21, 1991; U.N.G.A. Res. 46/137 (XLVI), December 17, 1991. See Franck, pp. 64–65.

explicitly committing to act to protect the terms of the settlement. International efforts to resolve the Salvadoran and Cambodian civil wars provide two examples.

In El Salvador, the Farabundo Martí National Liberation Front (FMLN) prepared to lay down its arms in early 1992 after a 12-year guerilla campaign against the government, in large part because of an implicit U.N. guarantee—symbolized by the presence of U.N. observers and police—that there would be strong international reaction if the Salvadoran army violated the terms of the settlement by arresting and torturing those who had been fighting against the government. The United Nations has such a substantial stake in the comprehensive settlement that crippling violations of the settlement might activate the Security Council and bring outside intervention. The parties signed the agreements knowing that the United Nations is capable of responding forcibly if the other side reneges.

The Cambodian agreement depends more explicitly on outside guarantees and assurances of support. Following two years of negotiations, the four parties in Cambodia's 13-year conflict, along with states participating in the Paris Conference on Cambodia, signed the Final Act of the Paris Conference on Cambodia on October 23, 1991.[29] The Paris Agreements called for an immediate ceasefire, demobilization of the rival armies, repatriation of 350,000 refugees, and elections by mid-1993. Under the settlement, the United Nations was charged with assuming the government's administrative duties, monitoring human rights, overseeing the return of refugees and the demobilization of the armies, and helping to organize the elections. The accords envision a democratic political structure with a 120-member assembly elected to draft and approve a constitution, to transform itself into a legislature, and to form a new Cambodian government. In addition to assigning tasks to the United Nations that would require an unprecedented level of U.N. involvement in areas normally considered to be part of a state's "internal" affairs, the accords commit the United Nations to responding if violations of the agreements occur.[30]

---

[29]Reprinted in *International Legal Materials*, vol. 31 (January 1992), pp. 174–204.

[30]See Article 5 of the "Agreement Concerning the Sovereignty, Independence, Territorial Integrity and Inviolability, Neutrality and National Unity of Cambodia," which called upon the treaty signatories to refer to the Security Council violations of the commitments of the agreement. In addition, in the event of human rights violations in Cambodia, the treaty signatories could call on the United Nations "to take such other steps as are appropriate for the prevention and suppression of such violations in accordance with the relevant international instruments." Reprinted in *International Legal Materials*, vol. 31 (January 1992), pp. 202–4.

Efforts to extend, consolidate, and defend democracy can cut both ways. The democratization process can often resolve self-determination claims by giving rise to a political system capable of protecting and accommodating groups that would otherwise be seeking changes in political arrangements or borders. But in other cases electoral democracy may not be enough. Democracy may mean little to a minority group that is constantly outvoted. It may mean little to an indigenous people whose political culture and traditions are different from those of other groups within the state. And it may mean little to a group that feels a historical claim entitles it to greater protection, more political power, or a state of its own.

Democracy and self-determination are interrelated and often compatible concepts. But the establishment of a democratic system will not always resolve a self-determination claim. Nor will the full exercise of self-determination always result in democracy. A major task for U.S. foreign policy and, more broadly, the international community is to perform the sometimes delicate balancing act between shepherding self-determination movements down democratic paths and acknowledging that democracy alone may not be enough to resolve self-determination claims.

The Law and Policy of Recognition

Recently, as discussed in Chapter Two, the United States and the European Community responded to the breakup of the Soviet Union and Yugoslavia by developing criteria for recognition of the successor states.[31] These criteria linked formal diplomatic recognition to the new state's specific commitments on its international behavior and treatment of its people. The criteria charted a new course for both the law and policy of recognition, but they also echoed important characteristics of earlier policies on recognition.

Recognition by the international community is essential to the ultimate survival of a self-determination movement whose aim is to break away from an existing state. The guidelines of international law on recognition of a political entity as they have evolved are often complex and imprecise.

---

[31]See pp. 27–38.

Nevertheless, it is useful to examine the evolution of international law and states' policies with respect to recognition.

Recognition of a State. International law makes an important distinction between recognition of a state and recognition of its government. In its widely respected treatise on U.S. foreign relations law, the American Law Institute defines a state as "an entity that has a defined territory and a permanent population, under the control of its own government, and that engages in, or has the capacity to engage in, formal relations with other such entities."[32] To recognize a state is to acknowledge that it possesses these characteristics; to recognize a government is to acknowledge a particular regime's control of that state.[33]

A government has some flexibility in the timing of its recognition of a new state. While formal recognition of an entity that meets the requisite criteria for statehood is not obligatory, governments have a duty to treat the qualifying entity as one entitled to the fundamental attributes of statehood under international law—such as respect for its territorial sovereignty and acknowledgement of the citizenship of its people. At the same time, states also have a duty not to recognize statehood too precipitously. During the breakup of a state, for example, the seceding entity or entities may require some period of scrutiny by other governments to determine whether the secession remains permanent and whether the criteria for statehood will be satisfied during the coming months and years.[34] International law also forbids recognition of an entity that has acquired the attributes of statehood because of an illegal threat or the use of military force.[35]

---

[32]American Law Institute, *Restatement of the Law Third: Restatement of the Foreign Relations Law of the United States*, vol. 1 (St. Paul: American Law Institute Publishers, 1987), sec. 201.

[33]An entity can be regarded as a state even if its precise boundaries are in dispute, it is under military occupation, the permanence of its population is strained by internal armed conflict or the migration of foreigners onto its territory, its government does not control every square mile of its territory, the conduct of its foreign affairs is delegated to a foreign power or to a multilateral institution, or it does not explicitly claim statehood.

[34]This is particularly important where the government of the "parent" state resists the attempt at secession. International recognition of statehood may be the critical factor in whether the entity attempting to secede makes the successful transition to independence.

[35]The U.N. Security Council can make this determination—as it did with Southern Rhodesia in Resolution 277 (March 18, 1970)—and compel member governments to deny recognition to a self-proclaimed state. In Resolution 662 (August 9, 1990), the Security Council directed all members not to recognize Iraq's annexation of Kuwait.

The real test of legitimacy for a new state, however, is its admission to multilateral institutions, particularly the United Nations. Article 4(1) of the U.N. Charter states that membership in the United Nations is open to "peace-loving states which accept the obligations contained in the present Charter and, in the judgment of the Organization, are able and willing to carry out these obligations." A state's application for U.N. membership must be approved by a majority vote of the 15-member Security Council (including either a favorable vote or abstention by each of the five permanent members) and a two-thirds vote of General Assembly members present and voting. In a strict sense, then, the United Nations is not a "universal" organization because its criteria for membership can result in the exclusion of states from the organization. Although a strict reading of Article 4(1) requires very little for a political entity to be admitted to the United Nations, in practice member states have often used additional political criteria to block the membership of states aligned with one superpower or the other.[36]

Recognition of a Government. The existence of a new state can be recognized without other governments extending diplomatic recognition to any government of that state. No government must, by law, formally recognize another government and establish diplomatic relations. That act remains discretionary, although it is expected that a regime that has effective control of a state is entitled to be treated as a government—whether or not formally recognized as such. Even when a government has been accorded formal recognition, other governments may decide—for political reasons—not to maintain diplomatic relations with that government.

International law does not impose firm criteria on any government with respect to its recognition policy toward other governments.[37] While some governments—such as the British government—generally have accorded

---

[36]Examples include a bloc of 16 states—each aligned with either the East or the West—finally admitted in 1955 after the superpower impasse was resolved, the People's Republic of China (admitted in 1973), North and South Korea (admitted in 1991), and Vietnam (blocked by the United States in 1975 and admitted in 1977).

[37]In 1950, the U.N. General Assembly debated the criteria for recognition of governments (in the context of representation of a member state in the United Nation) and ultimately recommended, in effect, no criteria at all. Recognition, it concluded, "should be considered in the light of the Purposes and Principles of the Charter and the circumstances of each case." U.N.G.A. Res. 396 (V), December 14, 1950; see Louis B. Sohn, *Cases in United Nations Law*, 2d ed. (Brooklyn: Foundation Press, 1967), pp. 113–15.

recognition to any government that has firmly established its control over the state's territory, in other states—and particularly in the United States— recognition practice has reflected a deeply political influence, often requiring fulfillment of political criteria by a government seeking recognition.[38]

In the early twentieth century, for example, the United States employed the so-called Wilsonian policy of recognition, which depended upon the existence of a "just" government resting "upon the consent of the governed."[39] Although that policy was abandoned when the United States recognized the government of the Soviet Union in 1931, political requirements again entered into U.S. policy after World War II, with recognition often turning on the simple issue of whether or not a government was communist in character. The U.S. nonrecognition of the People's Republic of China until 1979 was one manifestation of that policy.[40]

In 1970, the United States again shifted its policy. If a government to which the United States had extended recognition was replaced by another, U.S. recognition of the government (however constituted) of the state would remain standing, regardless of its new ideology or the degree of popular support it enjoyed. Even though the United States would thus recognize a successor government's effective control of a state, the United States could choose to break diplomatic ties with the new government.[41]

Neither international law nor the history of recognition policy supports an inevitable "right" of recognition for a self-determination movement seeking independent statehood. Still, most of the international community—and even the United States in the last two decades and in the period before World War II—minimized such factors as the type of government or its behavior

---

[38]See L. Thomas Galloway, *Recognizing Foreign Governments: The Practice of the United States* (Washington, D.C.: American Enterprise Institute, 1978).

[39]President Wilson's Statement of March 11, 1913. Reprinted in Green H. Hackworth, *Digest of International Law* (Washington, D.C.: U.S. Government Printing Office, 1943), p. 187.

[40]According to Secretary of State John Foster Dulles, recognition of the People's Republic of China would not serve the U.S. national interest. In 1957, he pronounced: "No government has a right to have recognition. It is a privilege that is accorded, and we accord it when we think it will fit in with our national interest, and if it doesn't, we don't accord it." Press Conference of March 13, 1957. Reprinted in *U.S. Department of State Bulletin*, vol. 36 (1957), p. 536.

[41]See "Diplomatic Recognition," *U.S. Department of State Bulletin*, vol. 77 (1977), pp. 462–63. Reprinted in John A. Boyd, *Digest of United States Practice in International Law 1977* (Washington, D.C.: U.S. Department of State, 1977), pp. 19–21.

toward its citizens as relevant to the decision to recognize a state or its government.[42]

The development of explicit recognition criteria in the cases of the successor states to the Soviet Union and Yugoslavia has begun to reverse this general practice and to inject a significant list of political conditions into policies of recognition. This departure from the practice of recent decades is impressive, but neither the criteria nor the general approach of the United States or the European Community are designed to address the diverse range of challenges posed by self-determination movements around the globe.

Thus, international law on recognition, minority rights, and support for democracy is evolving to address the new demands of self-determination. But the dominant view of contemporary international law remains unsympathetic to such developments. It will take the leadership of governments and multilateral institutions to advance the law beyond the presumptions of the Cold War. And it will not happen quickly. But the accelerated pace of world events in the aftermath of the Cold War suggest that such evolution will occur sooner than we could have imagined a short time ago.

---

[42]Nonetheless, communist governments in some states—such as Albania, Cuba, North Korea, and Vietnam—were determining factors in U.S. nonrecognition or, in the case of Cuba, denial of diplomatic relations.

Chapter Five

AFTER THE COLD WAR:
A NEW APPROACH TO
SELF-DETERMINATION

T he end of the Cold War has forced the world community to suddenly come to grips with numerous claims of peoples seeking self-determination in a variety of different contexts. The clear principles that guided the confrontation with the Soviet Union have expired, and it is no longer possible to hold that all existing states should remain united and that no changes in international borders should be contemplated.

The breakup of the Soviet Union and of Yugoslavia may turn out to be special cases. The very existence of the central government was challenged by established republics often possessing nominal autonomy as well as a constitutionally guaranteed right to secede. The issue became not whether one group of people could secede from a state but whether the central state would survive at all.

In these crises, the U.S. government and the international community opposed or stymied the efforts of "breakaway" states until it was no longer a viable policy. Once confronted with the imminent disappearance of the central government of the Soviet Union and with separate governments in control of territory in Yugoslavia, the United States and the European Community each developed a set of criteria that called for republics seeking recognition as independent states to commit to principles governing both internal politics and external relations.

An approach that addresses self-determination claims only after a ruling government collapses or a wide-scale conflict is underway is dangerous. The United States and the world community are left with a fait accompli and with little influence; a better approach would be to develop a set of principles that can inform a timely response to the spectrum of self-determination claims: anti-colonial, sub-state, trans-state, those of dispersed or indigenous peoples, and representative.

Those principles will confront, and be conditioned by, three inescapable realities. First, international law is at bottom the guardian of the global status quo, just as the law of any nation favors the domestic status quo. We discuss at some length in this book developments—some quite provocative—in international legal and political circles that may or may not become binding and enforceable international law in the years ahead.[1] It is inevitable that the political process of responding to self-determination claims will at times overreach established international law. Some of the principles we discuss in this book are intended to push the outer envelope of international law. But this also means that the principles sometimes may conflict with norms of law and hence be impractical and unwise to insist upon. We do not underestimate the difficulties of the exercise or the exceptions and qualifications that inevitably will be made.

A second related reality is that the fluidity of international politics after the Cold War argues against any rigid application of new principles about how to establish relations with the wide range of self-determination movements described in our global survey.[2] There will be cases in which an all-or-nothing application of the principles is not only unrealistic but unwise and ultimately destructive of self-determination itself. Therefore we are not suggesting that in every case every principle be applied. But there should be an effort to start with the full package and then determine which principles, if any, are totally unrealistic or even damaging to the successful resolution of the self-determination claim.

Third, the challenges of self-determination in the new world order cannot and should not be tackled all at once. This will be a multi-year process, much as the imposition of international human rights principles on all countries has taken many years—and there is hardly full compliance yet. We are not calling for immediate implementation of all aspects of the new approach discussed in this book. Nor are we proposing that the U.S. government overreach its own capabilities to address self-determination claims. But we do propose a conceptual framework within which to continue the

---

[1]See Chapters Four and Six.
[2]See pp. 123–160.

process begun with the recognition of the successor states of the Soviet Union and Yugoslavia.

So, while flexibility is an obvious requirement in any foreign policy, self-determination movements will require a more coherent and systematic response in the years ahead. Contradictory policies can invite chaos and violence. The ultimate objective of the United States and the international community must be to respond constructively to the will of the people and to prevent or, if necessary, stop armed conflict generated by the engine of self-determination.

The United States, by providing leadership for the world community, can play a critical role in resolving self-determination crises. In any particular situation the United States will need to determine early whether it will (a) remain neutral, (b) support efforts of the central government to block a self-determination claim, (c) pressure the central government to respond to the demands of minority groups and thus preserve and strengthen the existing state, (d) lend support to a self-determination movement and accord it some form of de facto recognition, (e) support distinct territorial autonomy, or (f) back secession, in the last case developing conditions for U.S. recognition of the new state and its government.

The success of the new states of the former Soviet Union, and several states of the former Yugoslavia, in gaining recognition from the United States will lead other such movements to seek U.S. support. Washington should take such requests seriously, not by necessarily supporting every self-determination movement, but by monitoring them, imposing conditions for U.S. contacts, and intervening with the ruling government when appropriate. There is a risk that U.S. willingness to support some self-determination movements could spur efforts that threaten U.S. interests or encourage actions that bring violent repression. Despite this danger, the case for the United States to adopt a more sympathetic policy toward self-determination movements is compelling.

The collapse of the Soviet Union and of Yugoslavia demonstrated that self-determination claims—of whatever character—cannot be ignored or suppressed indefinitely. Some claims have deep roots and broad support within the society. Support for the status quo can contribute—as it may have in the cases of the Baltics and Yugoslavia—to a central government's belief that it can use force to suppress self-determination movements without fear of international isolation or intervention. Failure to articulate a clear policy emphasizing the need for reconciliation can increase the danger of violence or repression.

Good faith efforts at accommodating self-determination claims within federal or other multiethnic structures should be supported before new states are created and international boundaries redrawn. The United States and the world community probably should have intervened diplomatically in defense of Yugoslavia's federal bargain when Serbian president Slobodan Milošević began to break that bargain in 1989 and 1990, stirring the fears of Yugoslavia's non-Serbs and adding fuel to secessionist sentiment.

Standards for Evaluating Self-Determination Movements

What general principles should inform us about self-determination claims and about the central governments challenged by those claims?

An Unbiased Attitude. The United States should abandon any bias in favor of the status quo and dismissive of the rights of self-determination movements. An unbiased attitude does not mean that the United States should support every movement that presents itself as embodying a "people" possessing a right of self-determination. The United States should consider each case on its merits, but should apply standards consistently. An unbiased attitude also does not mean that the United States should abandon efforts to resolve self-determination claims without advocating the creation of a new state.

Type of Self-Determination Claim. A major determining factor in the U.S. response to a self-determination movement should be that movement's character. The categories of self-determination claims set out in Chapter Three help to distinguish among different types of self-determination movements, each requiring different policy responses. Often one category cannot fully describe a self-determination claim; several categories may be required.

- *Anti-colonial self-determination.* The classification of a claim as a legitimate expression of anti-colonial self-determination imposes an obligation on the United States, as well as the rest of the international community, to work toward the political independence of the state or territory in question.

- *Sub-state self-determination.* Assessing and responding to the effort of a group within an existing state to protect its minority rights, to create a new political arrangement, or to secede can be a complex and subjective process. In the post–Cold War world, sub-state claims are proliferating, placing greater strains on central governments and greater demands on multilateral institutions and the international community at large. A sub-state claim should be considered in light of the historic, ethnic, religious, or economic dimensions of the group's dispute with the ruling government, and with awareness of the degree of protection, self-government, or independence that it seeks. Simply waiting for crises to erupt without examining a movement's legitimacy is, at the very least, shortsighted. Sub-state claims can lead to civil war and to the forced displacement of hundreds of thousands of civilians. A more comprehensive, forward-looking approach can help prevent armed conflicts and protect the U.S. interests that armed conflict could threaten.

- *Trans-state self-determination.* When a self-determination claim involves more than one state, the assessment is even more complex than with sub-state claims. Self-determination movements that cut across international borders will not easily elicit support from the U.S. government, because they can challenge the authority of at least two central governments. In many cases, the full accommodation of a trans-state movement's demands would require radical changes in the borders of more than one state—an outcome unlikely to be encouraged by the U.S. government. Nonetheless, the United States must not shy away from properly identifying, assessing, and acknowledging trans-state self-determination movements. Trans-state movements are perhaps the most dangerous and politically destabilizing type of self-determination claim, because they can more readily spark inter-state conflict and large-scale cross-border migrations.

- *Self-determination of dispersed peoples.* There are no simple remedies for accommodating the interests of an ethnic group that is dispersed with other groups in one or more states. The challenge may rest more with seeking the protection of minority rights within an existing state than with responding to secessionist pressures. The latter would prove impractical under most circumstances. The most effective way to head off a dispersed people's attempts to establish its own state—moves that could involve ethnic "cleansing" operations and illegal land grabs—is to guarantee individual and minority rights within existing state structures. The United States can help to ensure that those rights will be protected by identifying dispersed peoples making self-determination claims and then pressuring existing governments to ensure full human and political rights.

- *Indigenous self-determination.* It is often expedient to forget about those indigenous groups that possess a special claim to land and resources dating back hundreds or even thousands of years. The United States has often mistreated or ignored its own Native American tribes, numbering some 300 today. Even indigenous groups that have been assimilated into the political and economic structures of the countries they inhabit invoke the principle of self-determination in an effort to restore their pride and distinctive identities. But a government's treatment of its indigenous peoples—perhaps even more than its treatment of other groups—is usually regarded as a matter of domestic rather than international concern. Nonetheless, the United States should be prepared to respond sympathetically to indigenous claims, both within its own borders and in other countries. Although there will be an understandable tendency to defer to another government's jurisdiction over its indigenous communities, the United States has a responsibility to properly identify the existence of those communities and to acknowledge their rights under international law.
- *Representative self-determination.* Where there are significant popular pressures for the overthrow of a repressive and nondemocratic regime, particularly one engaged in human rights violations, the United States should determine how to advance the popular cause in accordance with international law.

Ruling Government's Conduct: Human and Minority Rights. Critical to the evaluation of a self-determination movement's legitimacy is an assessment of how the ruling government that it challenges treats its people. Where the claim is for a more representative government, the United States should evaluate the central government's human rights record and its commitment to democratic processes. For other claims, the degree of protection accorded to minorities under domestic and international law is also crucial. The claim of a self-determination movement facing repression may be more legitimate than the claim of a movement that is not. For example, a Quebec that has substantial political and cultural autonomy may have a lesser claim to independence than Iraqi Kurds who are denied both. But while the central government's treatment of its people is an important consideration in the evaluation of a self-determination claim, it is not dispositive. There could be other compelling reasons to back a self-determination claim or to withhold support from it.

U.S. engagement with self-determination movements will not necessarily mean support for the creation of an independent state for the people seeking self-determination. Indeed, in most cases the United States, other governments, and multilateral institutions will be disinclined to support the creation of new states, but rather will seek to persuade central governments to respect the rights of minority groups within their borders and to grant them a substantial degree of autonomy, perhaps in a federal structure. Concerted U.S. involvement, backed by the tacit threat that the United States might support a movement for independence and even withdraw recognition from the central government if it uses force to suppress a self-determination movement, is likely to be most effective in persuading the central government to take individual human rights and the aspirations of its minorities seriously. This will be especially true when the United Nations or a regional body backs these demands.

Historical Factors. Many movements for self-determination are ethnically based and seek independence for a "people" that was once independent or that has a long history of struggling for independence. These are important but not determinative factors. The United States should not support every long-struggling movement, nor should it necessarily reject a drive for independence because the movement lacks a historical basis or an ethnic component.

The history of how a particular region came to be incorporated into a larger state may also be relevant in deciding whether to support a self-determination claim. The United States should consider whether a territory was forcibly incorporated into an aggressor state, voluntarily joined the state, or never existed as an independent state. Instances in which the United States previously accepted a forcible incorporation (for example, East Timor into Indonesia and Tibet into China) may deserve reevaluation. Many states throughout the world were created through conquest. In other cases, the breakup of empires—including the Ottoman, the Austro-Hungarian, and the British—placed significant minority populations in successor states without giving them the opportunity to choose which states they wished to join.

The People's Choice. Determining to what extent a group claiming self-determination is supported by the people on whose behalf it speaks is a difficult task. The very act of demonstrating support for self-determination can invite repression. Ideally, the people should vote on their preferred form of government and statehood. Even if, for example, the U.S. government and an international or regional body conclude that independence may be appropriate for a group claiming sub-state self-determination, they should not support independence, per se, but rather the right of the people to determine its future freely by referendum or some other credible means.

There is no obviously "fair" way to structure a plebiscite when actors in the relevant community support different outcomes, from total independence to various forms of autonomy to maintenance of the status quo. If there are more than two choices on the ballot, disputes may arise about how they should be worded and whether a plurality is sufficient. Even if the only question is whether the region should be an independent state, other problems may arise, such as whether a majority vote is sufficient, whether only some super-majority can be taken as a true reflection of opinion, and whether a minimum turnout should be required.[3]

The United States and the international community can only press for some form of election or plebiscite conducted freely and with international supervision in which the people of a region can express their views. In the absence of elections or a plebiscite, the United States should look at other forms of popular expression to determine the will of the people. This might include mass demonstrations, an influential underground press, acts of civil disobedience, resistance to government control, and armed conflict or civil war. In the end, the United States and the international community should have a credible basis for reaching the conclusion that a convincing majority of the people claiming a right of self-determination have done so willingly and freely.

Conduct of the Self-Determination Movement. As critical to a self-determination movement's legitimacy as the degree of support it receives is the behavior of its leaders and its adherents. The United States should weigh whether members of the group are engaged in widespread human rights violations or if, for example, individual leaders are responsible for

---

[3]For an excellent discussion of plebiscites in the context of self-determination, see Harold S. Johnson, *Self-Determination within the Community of Nations* (Leyden: Sijthoff, 1967), pp. 71–98.

torturing their opponents.[4] A group that does not uphold general principles of human rights and democracy is not likely to deserve U.S. support.

The United States will want to consider whether a group has used or is using military force to advance its claim to self-determination. Although the use of force by a people seeking to throw off colonial rule may be permissible under international law, military force in connection with other acts of self-determination has not been sanctioned. Nonetheless, the United States should not necessarily reject a self-determination claim simply because a movement uses force against an oppressive central government. The degree of oppression may leave the movement no other choice. Nor should the United States give support to a movement simply because it appears to be gaining some success by the use of force. The United States must be careful not to require evidence of violence and disruption before taking a self-determination movement seriously. The consequence of such a stance would be to compel a movement to use force.

The justifiable application of military force remains the rare exception to the rule. In most cases, the United States will find the use of military force by either the government or the self-determination movement to be unjustifiable. In assessing the use of force by an insurgent movement claiming a right of self-determination, the United States should consider whether the movement lacks the opportunity to express its views through the political system and the extent to which it attacks civilians.

The United States should consider not only the movement's current conduct but also the commitments its leaders are prepared to make about how they will govern and how they will treat the citizens—including minorities—within the territory over which they seek greater control.

Potential for Violent Consequences. The United States will need to consider the potential consequences of a self-determination movement achieving its aim. Particularly if the aim is to break off and form an independent state, giving support may risk fueling an armed conflict. At some point, the safety of the people themselves may weigh more heavily than their political aspirations, requiring the latter to give way to the former for the time being.

---

[4]For example, see "U.S. Asks Angola Rebel to Explain Rights Abuses," *New York Times*, March 31, 1992, p. A5.

Fear of violence and armed conflict should not paralyze the U.S. government. Conflict may be more likely if tensions between a self-determination movement and its government go unaddressed and unresolved. Fear of conflict should neither prevent the evaluation of a self-determination movement nor deprive the movement of the recognition that it may well deserve. The prospect of a civil war, for example, may be a compelling reason for the United States to extend de facto recognition to the self-determination movement and to use its diplomatic clout with the central government and the international community in support of a peaceful secession before the situation deteriorates into warfare.

Evaluating these factors from a perspective that recognizes both the legitimacy and strength of self-determination movements and the desirability of maintaining an existing state, the United States needs to decide whether or not to become involved and, if so, to what end. The United States should seek to build a consensus within regional and international organziations for its position, but should not sacrifice its own judgment and principles if such a consensus fails to materialize. Nonetheless, there should be a heavy presumption against any physical intervention in support of a self-determination movement or to assist a government in suppressing such a movement unless U.S. actions are pursuant to a decision of the U.N. Security Council or an appropriate regional body.[5]

In evaluating self-determination movements, the U.S. government and the world community generally will reach a crossroads at which they must decide to remain neutral, support the preservation of an existing state within its current borders, or back the creation of a new independent state. Any of these decisions can result in a variety of strategies and outcomes. The consequences of each of these policy options are discussed below.

Preserving an Existing State

In many cases, self-determination movements will not be seeking independent statehood. These cases would appear to simplify the policy choices for the U.S. government. The United States would not have to decide whether

---

[5]For a discussion of the appropriate role of foreign intervention, see Chapter Six.

to oppose the central government over a matter of secession and perhaps intervene in support of the self-determination movement. Nor would it have to decide about recognition of a new state or a new government or about admission to multilateral institutions.

On closer examination, however, the policy choices are no less difficult. Taking any stance on the demands of a self-determination movement—whether those demands are for the devolution of governmental responsibilities, greater protection of minority rights, or some form of autonomous identity within a state—can place the United States in the position of "interfering" in the internal affairs of another state. Lending support to a self-determination movement will require the United States—whether through its own diplomatic efforts or through multilateral institutions—to pressure the central government to accommodate those demands.

Parts of the world community will be skeptical of any U.S. proposal to intervene, viewing it as a manifestation of American imperialism. Some will suspect that U.S. intervention is aimed at helping American business rather than at protecting a right of self-determination. For this reason, U.S. involvement to press a government to respond sympathetically to a self-determination movement must have international support and be in accordance with international law. Current developments in international law—including the changing attitude toward minority rights and the proposition that people have an "entitlement" to democratic governance—may lead over time to the development of international law establishing the legitimacy of international and regional involvement in self-determination disputes.

A broad U.S. policy supporting the preservation of existing states that accommodates the interests (excluding secession) of self-determination movements would differ sharply from a neutral policy of acquiescence in the fate of self-determination claims within foreign countries. With the former approach, the United States would become more active than it has been in pressing the case for protection of minority rights and for devolution of governmental power, in the belief that such initiatives are necessary to prevent the breakup of an existing state and are worthy goals in and of themselves.

Because there are real costs to the creation of new states, and there can be even higher costs to frustrating and repressing self-determination claims, there is a clear need for earlier involvement by governments and multilateral institutions to try to satisfy self-determination claims within the context of the existing state. Federalism is an attractive means of addressing self-determination claims. The Canadian, Indian, and Nigerian federal systems are important, albeit imperfect, examples.

A more difficult situation arises when a self-determination movement advocates secession but the U.S. government supports the preservation of the existing state. In those cases in which the United States believes that the self-determination movement has credible claims against the central government short of secession, the challenge will be to press for protection of the group's minority rights and some degree of self-government despite the group's more far-reaching aspirations. The central government should commit to treating its citizens, including those making a self-determination claim, in accordance with international law, particularly principles of human and minority rights.

As noted earlier, the United States or other countries should not provide active support for an independence movement without first seeking to persuade the central government to take steps short of granting independence to deal with the demands. If the United States and the appropriate multilateral institution conclude that an independence movement has popular support but has not yet made the case for separation from the state, it should insist that the government blocking the independence movement live up to the criteria for the relationship between a government and its people suggested below for new states. Thus, a state resisting a separatist self-determination claim should move toward a constitutional democracy with genuinely free elections, respect for political opposition, limits on the police power of the state, and respect for individual human rights and minority rights. If, over time, a state is unable or unwilling to move in this direction, the case grows stronger for supporting a separatist self-determination movement that commits itself to creating such a government, and, as discussed below, permitting an international response if that government fails to live up to these commitments.

Supporting the Emergence of a New State

Assuming the U.S. government decides that the time has come to consider supporting a claim to independent statehood, what should the United States require of a new government before it recognizes its legitimacy?

We argue that the United States, preferably joined by other countries and appropriate multilateral institutions, should seek specific commitments from a self-determination movement before supporting its cause and later from a new government before establishing diplomatic relations.

As the United States and the international community approach decisions on recognition, they must be prepared to handle three types of situations. First, in some instances, a historically constituted republic or former state within an existing state will secede and immediately acquire the attributes of statehood. This was the case when the twelve non-Baltic republics of the former Soviet Union achieved independence upon the formal termination of the central government on December 25, 1991, by Soviet president Mikhail Gorbachev. The total collapse of a central government poses a relatively rare set of circumstances, with new states appearing before governments can meet recognition criteria. States and governments do not necessarily acquire legitimacy co-terminously. This does not diminish the value or necessity of recognition criteria for the new government; it simply means that the reality of the new state will be acknowledged or recognized before the new government is granted formal recognition. Nor does the prospect that a central government will collapse—leading to the sudden emergence of new states—diminish the value or necessity of seeking commitments from self-determination movements.

A second set of circumstances exists in those cases where recognition of a new government precedes the creation or recognition of a new state. This could happen when the central government's troops occupy the territory claimed by the new government and control access to and from that territory. The situation in Lithuania, Estonia, and Latvia during 1990 and 1991 exemplifies this dilemma, albeit under unique circumstances.[6] Many states now recognize a government for the Palestinian people even though it has no control over the territory it claims.

The third and most likely situation is simultaneous recognition of a new state and its government. The Yugoslav experience is an example of how intertwined the fate of a new state can be with the international

---

[6]For example, the United States could have formally restored diplomatic ties and working relationships with the Baltic governments-in-exile represented at legations in the United States. This might have been particularly useful in response to Soviet military intimidation of the Baltic nations.

legitimacy of its new government. The European Community recognized the statehood of two of the seceding republics, Slovenia and Croatia, and their new governments simultaneously. Three months later, the Community simultaneously recognized the statehood and government of Bosnia-Herzegovina. In effect, in all three cases, the legitimacy of the new states remained in suspension until their new governments had committed to the recognition criteria set out by the European Community. In the case of the fourth republic seeking independence, Macedonia, legitimacy remained in suspension even longer. Greek concerns that its very use of the name "Macedonia" implied territorial ambitions prompted the European Community and the United States to withhold recognition of its statehood and of its government in spite of its government's repeated commitments to the relevant criteria.[7]

What is clear in all of these cases is the need to impress upon a self-determination movement the importance of an early commitment to recognition criteria. At a minimum, the leaders of the movement should sign a commitment letter affirming the intention of their group to abide by the recognition criteria once a government is formed to rule the emerging state. When and if the newly constituted government seeks recognition, a second commitment letter will need to be drawn up and signed by the duly authorized officials of the new government. This second commitment letter will require more detailed and comprehensive pledges.

Criteria for Transition to Independent Statehood

A major weakness of the international community's response to self-determination claims thus far has been the lack of coordination. The United States, other concerned governments, and an appropriate international organization should arrive at a reasonable set of principles to which a self-determination movement should commit before being granted support or recognition as a newly formed government. In some cases, that formal

---

[7]"Greece Blocks Recognition of Macedonia," *Washington Post*, June 10, 1992, p. A25.

commitment should entail granting to a specified international or regional body the right to intervene to ensure compliance with those principles.

The following principles are not necessarily exhaustive in scope, but provide criteria against which to judge whether to recognize both the newly created state and the specific government in charge.

U.N. Standards of Admission. The first set of criteria already exists in Article 4(1) of the U.N. Charter. The standards for admission of a state to the United Nations require that the state be "peace-loving," accept the obligations in the U.N. Charter, and be "able and willing to carry out these obligations." As the interpretation and application of the Charter evolve in the post–Cold War era, these obligations will broaden and deepen. More explicit commitments should be obtained, as explained below, with regard to Charter obligations regarding the rule of international law, the inviolability of borders, and the non-use of force.

Adherence to International Law. The leaders of a self-determination movement and of a new government they create must pledge to adhere to the general principles of international law. In addition, they must commit to upholding the specific international legal obligations of the predecessor state. International law consists of both a large body of customary norms that in the view of many scholars would automatically bind any newly emerging state[8] and numerous treaties and conventions, many of which may not bind either the predecessor state or the newly emerging state. Therefore, a pledge by a self-determination movement and by any new government that may emerge will need to be specific with respect to what codified international law will be endorsed and comprehensive enough to guarantee the rights and obligations found in customary international law.[9]

---

[8]See American Law Institute, *Restatement of the Law Third: Restatement of the Foreign Relations Law of the United States,* vol. 1 (St. Paul: American Law Institute Publishers, 1987), sec. 102, comment d; Michel Virally, "The Sources of International Law," in *Manual of Public International Law*, ed. Max Sorenson (New York: St. Martin's Press, 1968), pp. 132 and 137–39.

[9]See *Restatement of the Law Third,* vol. 1, sec. 210(3) and (4):
(3) When part of a state becomes a new state, the new state does not succeed to the international agreements to which the predecessor state was party, unless, expressly or by implication, it accepts such agreements and the other party or parties thereto agree or acquiesce.
(4) Pre-existing boundary and other territorial agreements continue to be binding notwithstanding [subsection (3)].

But compare with Article 34 of the Vienna Convention on Succession of States in Respect of Treaties (1978), reprinted in Marian Lloyd Nash, *Digest of United States Practice in International Law 1978* (Washington, D.C.: U.S. Department of State, 1980), p. 717.

Inviolability of Borders. The emergence of any new state will require changes in international borders. Sometimes the new international boundaries will reflect existing divisions among republics, as occurred with the breakup of the Soviet Union. But even as international borders are created between a breakaway entity and its parent state or among successor states, other international boundaries remain inviolable. An emerging state is not free to readjust its borders with a neighboring country without its consent. A self-determination movement and any new government must explicitly recognize and respect existing international boundaries and internal borders dividing distinct republics or territories and agree that either type of border can be changed only through peaceful and consensual means. By using force to change such borders, a self-determination movement or a new government will forfeit U.S. support.

When the international community backs the emergence of a new state, it does not necessarily accept the boundaries that a self-determination movement seeks to establish. In many cases, there will be areas where there is no accepted boundary between the region seeking independence and the rest of the original state. In other cases, the traditional boundary may no longer reflect the actual distribution of the population. A new state may have areas inhabited in large part by the ethnic group that makes up the majority in the original state.

In such situations, the United States and the international community should consider backing a political arrangement that makes a distinction between "citizenship" and "territory." This arrangement would permit people living in a designated area to choose in which of the contiguous countries they wish to hold citizenship. Such areas would need to have substantial local autonomy; functions that must be performed centrally could be placed under the joint control of the two governments. Where necessary, an international force could be stationed on the territory to ensure that the rights of all people are respected. While this concept poses very real difficulties, it deserves serious consideration in the context of ethnic disputes that cannot be settled simply by drawing a border between states.

Non-Use of Force. In support of the requirement of Article 4(1) that states admitted to the United Nations be "peace-loving," a self-determination movement and, prior to recognition, a new government should be required to commit to existing international regimes, as well as treaties adhered to by the parent state, that limit the use of force and the size and structure of military services.

More specifically, a new government should be required to:

a) agree that it will not seek to use force to settle any boundary dispute or to resolve any irredentist claim. A new government should agree to resolve such disputes by peaceful means including, if necessary, submitting the matter to mediation, conciliation, arbitration, the International Court of Justice, or—in circumstances of armed conflict or potential armed conflict—the U.N. Security Council or relevant regional body;

b) adhere to the Nuclear Non-Proliferation Treaty as a non-nuclear state and sign a comprehensive inspection agreement with the International Atomic Energy Agency; and

c) accept limits on the size of conventional military forces that are consistent both with self-defense requirements and with a commitment to resolve disputes by peaceful means, to use force only in self-defense or as part of an action of collective security, and to comply with the procedural requirements of the U.N. Charter and the charter of any relevant regional organization to confront aggression by other states. The precise nature of this commitment would depend on the particular situation, including the nature of any arms control agreements to which the parent state might have adhered, the size and disposition of the military forces of the parent state and surrounding states, and the potential military threat that neighboring states may pose.

Peaceful Settlement of Disputes. A new government must commit to peaceful settlement of internal and international disputes. The international system provides a number of forums in which disputes can be addressed through negotiation, mediation, conciliation, arbitration, and adjudication. A new government engaged in either internal or external aggression fails the test of legitimacy in the new world order. A new government can best demonstrate its commitment to the peaceful settlement of disputes by joining relevant arbitration conventions and submitting to the compulsory jurisdiction of the International Court of Justice (ICJ). Unfortunately, the United States no longer submits to the compulsory jurisdiction of the ICJ and thus is in a weak position to insist that any other state do so.[10] If the United

---

[10]The United States formally terminated its submission to the compulsory jurisdiction of the ICJ on October 7, 1985, effective as of April 7, 1986. See *International Legal Materials*, vol. 24 (November 1985), pp. 1742–1745.

States were to return to the compulsory jurisdiction of the ICJ, that action would encourage new governments to use the Court for adjudication of particularly complex or volatile disputes that otherwise might trigger armed conflict.[11]

Constitutional Democracy. The United States should not formally recognize a new government unless its commitment to democracy is clear and strong. The United States should encourage newly emerging states to establish "limited" constitutional democracy as their form of government. That term refers, in general, to a regime that draws its legitimacy from the people through elections, based on a constitution specifying the powers of state institutions, and that limits the state's right to interfere with the actions of its citizens.

A group making a self-determination claim and seeking international and U.S. support should conduct its internal affairs, such as the selection of its leadership, as much as possible according to democratic processes.[12] It should also formally pledge to adopt a written constitution guaranteeing democracy and limiting governmental power if and when it takes control in an independent state.

Periodic free elections are the cornerstone of any commitment to democracy. To be free, an election should have the following characteristics:

a) all adult citizens of the state must have the right to vote. The determination of who qualifies to be a citizen in a new state can prove to be a discriminatory and undemocratic process. For example, the Russian minorities in the Baltic countries and other successor states of the Soviet Union often have been excluded from the electoral processes of their newly-constituted states. It may prove necessary to discourage and, if necessary, hold up recognition of a new state or penalize a recognized new state for engaging in such discriminatory practices;

---

[11]U.N. secretary-general Boutros Boutros-Ghali called upon all states to accept the general, or compulsory, jurisdiction of the ICJ, without any reservation, by the year 2000, in his report *An Agenda for Peace*, U.N.G.A. A/47/277 (June 17, 1992), U.N. Sec. Council S/24111 (June 17, 1992), pars. 38, 39. Reservations, however, have been and probably will be required by many states, including the United States, before they submit to the Court's compulsory jurisdiction.

[12]The internationally observed elections for a national assembly and leader held in the Kurdish area of northern Iraq, although under allied air protection, provide one example. See "To the Kurds, Wistful Wish Becomes Real," *New York Times*, May 20, 1992, p. A6; "Heavy Turnout, Calm Mark Kurds' First Vote," *Washington Post*, May 20, 1992, p. A25.

b) any group of citizens must have the right to form a political party and to compete on an equal basis in the election;

c) there must be a secret ballot that is free of intimidation or fraud;

d) international observers must be permitted to be present in the country during the election and to certify the accuracy of the vote count;

e) the party winning the election must have the right to form a government with the real power to govern the nation. More specifically, the military cannot have a de facto ability to run the country regardless of who wins the election; and

f) the periodic holding of free elections must be embodied in the constitution of the state. It is not sufficient that a state has held one free election but made no institutional arrangement for subsequent periodic elections.

This last point is perhaps the most important and underscores the need for commitments to a "limited" constitutional democracy rather than simply a democracy. The adoption of a constitution ensures that an elected leader, even one chosen overwhelmingly in a free election, is not free to end the process of free elections or to eliminate the other rights discussed below. Few nations meet the standards for a constitutional democracy as outlined here. However, these standards are becoming more common, and the United States and the world community should exact them as the price of supporting a group seeking to create a new state.

Right of Political Dissent. To make the commitment to free elections credible, a new state's constitution must also guarantee a right of political dissent. People must have the right, free from the fear of arrest, to express their opposition to the government and its policies and actions. They must have the ability to communicate these views to others through such means as freedom of the press and assembly. The state must not be able to prevent the expression of dissident views on radio and television. Independent political organizations and parties must have the right to form, to function freely, and to communicate with sympathetic groups and individuals throughout the world. Above all, the legitimacy of political dissent must be accepted by the government of the day and must be clearly enshrined in the basic law of the land. There must be an independent judiciary capable of enforcing these and other rights.

Protection of Individual and Minority Rights. The constitution of the new state must provide protection for the rights of individuals and, if appropriate, of minority groups. Individual rights include the right of political dissent (discussed above), the right to be free of arbitrary police power (discussed below), as well as such other internationally recognized rights as the right to form a trade union and to strike, the right to cultural freedom, the right to travel, and the right to exchange ideas across state borders.[13] Minority rights need not include the right to a veto over the state decisions or the right of political autonomy. However, they do need to go beyond guaranteeing the individual freedoms of each member of the minority and provide that a group sharing ethnic, linguistic, religious, or cultural bonds is entitled to respect for its distinctive status and to such guarantees as freedom of religion, the ability to educate its children in separate schools, and the freedom to organize political parties and to compete in elections. If the minority lives in a distinct geographic area, guarantees of local political autonomy and even the adoption of a federal structure may be appropriate.

Limits on Arbitrary Police Power. In order to ensure rights for all people, a new government must enact limits on the right of the police to arrest people and to hold them without public charges and a trial. The constitution of the new state does not need to include all the protections of the U.S. constitution. In fact, additional protections can be found in international instruments. But the constitution must prohibit torture, require that persons held be publicly charged within a specified period for a specific crime, and establish some mechanism permitting early judicial review of the legitimacy of any detention. Both domestic and international human rights groups must be afforded reasonable access to prisoners.

Market-Oriented Economy. The United States required movement toward a free-market economy and free and fair trade in its recognition criteria for the successor states of the Soviet Union.[14] However, it is more appropriate to include such criteria as a condition for American economic assistance

---

[13]International Covenant on Civil and Political Rights, U.N.G.A. Res. 2200A (XXI), adopted December 16, 1966, and entered into force March 23, 1976; Conference on Security and Cooperation in Europe, "Document of the Copenhagen Meeting of the Conference on the Human Dimension of the CSCE," June 29, 1990. Reprinted in *International Legal Materials*, vol. 29 (September 1990), pp. 1305–1322.

[14]In his December 12, 1991, speech at Princeton University, Secretary of State James Baker called upon entities seeking ties to the United States to "commit to responsible security policies, democratic political practices, and free-market economics." Reprinted in *U.S. Department of State Dispatch*, vol. 2 (1991), p. 890.

and for U.S. support for assistance from international financial institutions than for recognition per se. Although it is unlikely that any new state would adopt the rigid centralized planning structures that characterized the Soviet Union, there are a number of alternatives that could combine market-oriented economics and state regulation. Support for a self-determination movement or recognition of a new government need not depend on an explicit commitment to a plan for economic reform that U.S. or international experts feel is most likely to be effective. Such demands would increase the fear of other states that this entire scheme is simply an elaborate justification for U.S. imperialism. At the same time, such demands are perfectly legitimate as the price of international economic assistance, as the practice of the International Monetary Fund illustrates.

Enforcement Mechanism. An important gap in the criteria enunciated by the United States and the European Community is the absence of a requirement allowing external enforcement of those criteria. This is not surprising in view of the controversial nature of any "right" of the international community to intervene in a state—even if intervention is based on a government's consent. In some cases, enforcement may simply be unrealistic. But the United States should not abandon the requirement in any particular case without first determining that a new government is likely to honor its commitments to the other criteria and that no threat to the government exists that would hamper its ability to do so.

In most cases, the United States and the international community should require commitments—first from a self-determination movement and later from any new government that emerges from the struggle for statehood—that would explicitly authorize the international community, through the U.N. Security Council or a regional organization, to intervene in the new state for only a stipulated period of time (perhaps a maximum of five years) in order to guarantee adherence to the recognition criteria.[15]

A new government seeking international recognition on the basis of a claim of self-determination would in effect accept the authority of the Security Council or a regional body to guarantee a limited constitutional democracy—that is, to ensure that the state lives up to its commitments to

---

[15]The character of the intervention can range from diplomatic intervention to military intervention depending upon the nature and magnitude of the state's action or inaction with respect to the recognition criteria.

its people and to the world community about how it will treat persons within its territory.

The introduction of an enforcement mechanism is a radical proposal that raises the question of why a small number of new states would agree to such an intrusive instrument, when all existing and even some other new states would not be subject to its requirements. There is no easy or equitable answer, but if the growing global commitment to humanitarian imperatives and democratic principles makes it possible to impose requirements in these areas as a condition for recognition, the world community must have a means of ensuring that they are met.

The proliferation of self-determination claims in the post–Cold War world imposes considerable strain on the international political system. We have argued that there is an obligation on the part of the United States and other countries to take self-determination seriously and even to support the creation of new states where it is warranted. But it would be unacceptable for the United States in particular to maintain a policy of support if a new state reneged on its commitments and subjected its people to violations of human, civil, minority, and political rights. Self-determination movements and new governments cannot commit to these rights one day only to be free to violate them the next. An international enforcement mechanism to guarantee these rights is in the interest of the people of a new state.

There are a number of historical precedents for this kind of enforcement mechanism. The legal regime for the protection of minority rights established by the League of Nations pursuant to treaties with several new or reconfigured states in Europe had no effective enforcement mechanism and ultimately collapsed.[16] Since then, acceptance of the idea that international and regional bodies have a role in assuring that a new state and its government live up to commitments to function as a limited constitutional democracy has grown. As the Security Council, various U.N. bodies, and regional organizations in Europe and Latin America are getting involved in resolving internal disputes of other states, they are implicitly, and to some degree explicitly, taking on the right and commitment to intervene to protect the terms of the settlement. The international settlements in El Salvador and Cambodia seem to contemplate such intervention.[17]

---

[16]See pp. 54–56.
[17]See pp. 60–65.

Nonetheless, the implementation of enforcement mechanisms can be fraught with uncertainties and political impotence. In mid-1992, the United Nations faced defiance of its mandates in Bosnia-Herzegovina, Iraq, and Cambodia. The credibility of an international authority to enforce international law and the will of the Security Council hung in the balance.[18]

This chapter sets forth standards and criteria to better inform government analysts and policymakers as they respond to the growing number of self-determination movements claiming the right to form a new state. These factors can also provide more guidance to those participating in the movements, for the legitimacy and ultimate success of any self-determination claim to the right to establish a new state will rest in large part on the issues that frame these standards and criteria. The objective is not to stultify the creativity of the U.S. government or other governments in their response to particular self-determination claims, but to broaden and deepen the analytic framework and help policymakers make wiser decisions.

[18]Jeane Kirkpatrick, "The Only Way to Stop Aggression," *Washington Post*, August 3, 1992, p. A19.

Chapter Six

RESPONDING TO
INTERNATIONAL HOT SPOTS

S elf-determination is not a self-regulating process; nor is it necessarily a peaceful endeavor. The quest for self-determination can breed horrific violence, oppressive dictatorships, humanitarian crises, and large-scale warfare. "Internal" military conflicts can quickly bring threats to international peace and security, including mass migrations, widespread human rights violations, arms transfers, cross-border combat, and economic disruptions. It would be irresponsible for the world community to stand by idly and watch medieval carnage consume both old and new states in the years ahead.

Collective use of military force to enforce international law and the resolutions of the Security Council will become more familiar in the years ahead. During the Cold War, the world became accustomed to thinking of the use of military force only in terms of aggression or self-defense. The American aim, whether overtly in Korea, Vietnam, or Grenada, or covertly in Nicaragua, Angola, Afghanistan, or Cambodia, was often to contain or roll back communism. The notion that applying military force collectively to uphold principles of international law and to discipline nations had not taken hold, although it was envisaged by the drafters of the U.N. Charter.[1]

Defending the new world order will demand the collective use of military force, particularly to deal with the violent convulsions of some self-determination claims. This will require the political will to use military force for novel purposes: to defend democracy from violent overthrow, to protect

---

[1] See U.N. Charter, Chapter VII, particularly Articles 42-50. See also D.W. Bowett, *United Nations Forces* (New York: Praeger, 1964).

the human rights of large groups of people (notably minorities) from egregious violations, to end humanitarian nightmares, or to stop a devastating civil war. Forging a consensus on how and under what circumstances to use such force is a precondition for the development of that political will. Part of that consensus is a recognition that the United States cannot, will not, and should not intervene militarily in all or even most conflicts arising from self-determination claims. Judgments will have to be reached as to the priority to accord to various conflicts, where the humanitarian imperative is the greatest, and what collective mechanism—regional or international—will best meet the need for action.

At the same time there are, to be sure, other responses to self-determination short of military force that should be tried first, if possible. These include monitoring, diplomatic pressures, denial of international legitimacy, conditionality in development assistance, and economic sanctions.

This chapter discusses recent developments in each of these areas and their possible roles in dealing with self-determination claims. We confine our discussion to the "hot spots"—that is, those situations in which a peaceful resolution of a self-determination claim fails, and the situation threatens to deteriorate into armed conflict or a humanitarian crisis.

Monitoring

Throughout the world, international and regional organizations are creating means to monitor matters relating to self-determination in newly emerging states. Through its peacekeeping and observer missions in a small but growing number of states, the United Nations monitors compliance with cease-fires, oversees referenda and elections, and in some cases even administers a transitional government.[2] Where a U.N. peacekeeping force operates in the middle of a civil war, as in Bosnia-Herzegovina, it ends up monitoring the conflict.

---

[2]See United Nations, *The Blue Helmets: A Review of United Nations Peacekeeping* (New York: United Nations, 1990), pp. 313–402; United Nations, *United Nations Electoral Assistance to Haiti* (New York: U.N. Department of Public Information, 1991); United Nations, *Election Supervision: The United Nations Experience in Namibia and Nicaragua* (New York: U.N. Department of Public Information, 1990).

The Conference on Security and Cooperation in Europe has taken several steps toward a permanent monitoring capacity in its member states, particularly those where nationalism and ethnic rivalries are generating armed conflicts. In October 1991, representatives from the CSCE member states adopted a far-reaching document on the "human dimension" that, among other initiatives, establishes procedures for assigning human rights experts to fact-finding missions within member states to investigate human rights, fundamental freedoms, democracy, and the rule of law.[3] CSCE human rights rapporteurs visited all of the non-Baltic successor states of the Soviet Union. The governments' respective agreements to accept the rapporteurs were at least a tacit condition of CSCE membership. This can serve as a useful precedent for the monitoring that may need to be done in newly emerging states. These CSCE missions will be directly involved in issues arising from self-determination claims. In July 1992, the CSCE created the job of High Commissioner on National Minorities, an independent figure who should be of international repute. The High Commissioner "will have considerable latitude to investigate situations on the ground, mediate between the parties, and make recommendations to the CSCE's governing councils. If given the proper support, he (or she) could really help nip conflicts in the bud."[4]

Many governments, multilateral institutions, and private bodies carry out a wide range of monitoring activities across the globe. In addition to the many groups that participate regularly in monitoring elections and human rights,[5] a smaller number of groups monitor the transfer and development of arms[6] and the growth of democracy.[7] This de facto monitoring network can have a significant influence on identifying and responding to self-determination claims and influencing the new governments that emerge from such claims.

---

[3]Conference on Security and Cooperation in Europe, "Document of the Moscow Meeting of the Conference on the Human Dimension of the CSCE." Reprinted in *International Legal Materials*, vol. 30 (November 1991), p. 1670.

[4]David Shorr, "Plenty of Work Ahead For a Beefed-Up CSCE," *Christian Science Monitor*, July 14, 1992, p. 18.

[5]See Amnesty International, *Report 1992* (New York: Amnesty International USA, 1992); House Committee on Foreign Affairs and Senate Committee on Foreign Relations, *U.S. Department of State Country Reports on Human Rights Practices for 1991*, 102d Cong., 2d sess., Joint Committee Print.

[6]See, for example, Leonard S. Spector, *Nuclear Ambitions* (Boulder: Westview Press, 1990).

[7]See R. Bruce McColm et al., *Freedom in the World: Political Rights & Civil Liberties 1991–1992* (New York: Freedom House, 1992).

These existing monitoring activities are important, but more needs to be done. The U.S. government, which has no agency or even individual charged with monitoring self-determination movements, should approach self-determination more systematically by establishing its own monitoring capability. The State Department should prepare an annual report similar to the annual human rights reports mandated by Congress since 1977,[8] which would identify and analyze self-determination movements in all countries. Alternatively, the annual human rights report could incorporate information on self-determination claims. (The global survey of self-determination movements in the appendix of this book offers one way to start thinking about such a report.) As the years progress, this body of information would enhance the government's ability to respond to crises and to develop constructive policies toward the self-determination movements, the governments they challenge, and the new governments that may emerge from their efforts.

Diplomatic Intervention

When governments and multilateral institutions speak of peacefully resolving disputes arising out of self-determination claims, they have in mind—first and foremost—diplomacy. Negotiations between the parent government and the leaders of the self-determination movement are an essential first step. This early stage offers the best opportunity for a government to negotiate and formulate new policies to address the concerns of a self-determination movement in ways that will preserve the existing state.

When diplomacy fails, the parties to an internal dispute over self-determination can turn to third-party mechanisms to help reach a settlement. These familiar mechanisms include mediation, conciliation, arbitration, and adjudication.

Mediation is perhaps the most useful means to bridge the gap between recalcitrant government officials and minority leaders. The CSCE has pushed this concept furthest in recent years. In February 1991, a CSCE meeting of experts issued a report recommending in part the creation of a CSCE

---

[8]See Sections 116(d) and 502B(b) of the Foreign Assistance Act of 1961, as amended; 22 U.S.C. 2151n. and 22 U.S.C. 2304.

Dispute Settlement Mechanism to offer "comment or advice" to disputing parties on "suitable procedures for the settlement of the dispute."[9] Although the CSCE mechanism is intended to deal with conflicts between states, it encourages mediation or other forms of dispute settlement for ethnic conflicts that cut across international boundaries. The CSCE mechanism, however, does not impose mandatory procedures on parties to reach a peaceful settlement. Significantly, the CSCE mechanism does not require a party to pursue these peaceful dispute settlement procedures if the case "raises issues concerning its territorial integrity, or national defence, title to sovereignty over land territory, or competing claims with regard to the jurisdiction over other areas."[10] The CSCE launched an eleven-nation conference in 1992 to mediate the armed conflict between Armenia and Azerbaijan over the fate of Nagorno-Karabakh. The participants' hidden agenda may have been to exclude Iran from influencing the outcome of the dispute, and the CSCE's ability to resolve the matter remained dubious in mid-1992.[11] In the future, the CSCE's new High Commissioner on National Minorities will be able to undertake mediating duties.

Mediation played a major role in attempts to end the conflicts that erupted in Croatia and Bosnia-Herzegovina in 1991 and 1992. Former U.S. Secretary of State Cyrus Vance was asked by the U.N. secretary-general to mediate the conflict in Croatia. His efforts contributed to an ultimate cease-fire in Croatia (where at least 10,000 died) and the deployment of a sizable U.N. peacekeeping force there.[12] Bosnia-Herzegovina did not fare as well. U.N. and EC mediation proved largely futile. Vance was again sent as the U.N. secretary-general's envoy to South Africa in mid-1992 to assess the increasingly volatile situation there.

Conciliation services and arbitration panels could also be useful tools to reach peaceful accommodations between self-determination movements and parent governments. The CSCE, for example, is considering a Franco-German proposal to create a Court of Conciliation and Arbitration. The

---

[9]"Report of the CSCE Meeting of Experts on Peaceful Settlement of Disputes, Valletta 1991." Reprinted in *International Legal Materials*, vol. 30 (March 1991), p. 392.

[10]CSCE, "Peaceful Settlement of Disputes," p. 393.

[11]Paul A. Goble, "Coping with the Nagorno-Karabakh Crisis," *Fletcher Forum*, vol. 16 (Summer 1992), pp. 24–26.

[12]See U.N. Sec. Council Resolution 743 (XLVI), February 21, 1992.

United States has suggested a mechanism for the CSCE that would be less binding than arbitration.

While resort to the International Court of Justice (ICJ) would be infrequent, the ICJ can play a useful role in resolving some of the thorny legal issues that arise in self-determination claims, particularly to clarify the authority of a parent government and the rights of a self-determination movement. Both the Security Council and the General Assembly are empowered to request advisory opinions from the ICJ.[13] This advisory function permits the United Nations to bring to the ICJ for its opinion a self-determination claim that may be confined to one state, even though such a claim may not be admissible before the Court as a legal dispute. The ICJ's advisory opinion on the status of the Western Sahara in 1975 established the legal basis upon which a self-determination claim has been pursued there. In that opinion, the Court found no legal impediments to the application of General Assembly Resolution 1514 (XV) in the decolonization of the Western Sahara or of the principle of self-determination for the people of that territory.[14] Similarly, where two states are in dispute over a claim of self-determination, the ICJ can serve as a legal arena in which to adjudicate and settle the dispute.

The ICJ can invoke a special "chambers" procedure whereby a small panel of ICJ judges considers an application rather than the usual sitting of all 15 judges.[15] Parties in a particular dispute might feel more comfortable submitting their disputes to a panel whose composition they approve of in advance.[16] Alternatively, the ICJ could designate a few judges who would be willing to specialize on self-determination issues and establish a standing chamber to handle self-determination disputes.[17] Similar resort to adjudication on self-determination claims might be initiated in Europe before the European Court of Human Rights or the European Court of Justice.

---

[13]The U.N. secretary-general has proposed that his office be granted the power to request advisory opinions from the ICJ. See Boutros Boutros-Ghali, *An Agenda for Peace*, U.N.G.A. A/47/277 (June 17, 1992), U.N. Sec. Council S/24111 (June 17, 1992), par. 38.

[14]Advisory Opinion concerning *Western Sahara*, ICJ REPORTS 1975, p. 12.

[15]ICJ Statute, Articles 26-29.

[16]The United States and Italy used the chambers approach in *Elettronica Sicula S.p.A. (ELSI) (United States v. Italy)*, ICJ REPORTS 1989, p. 15.

[17]See ICJ Statute, Article 26.

Denial of International Legitimacy

The international community has two ways of denying legitimacy—derecognition and suspension or expulsion from international institutions. Derecognition involves a government terminating diplomatic relations, withdrawing its diplomatic personnel, and expelling the offending government's diplomats.[18] Derecognition might be taken further to explicitly deny the offending government any legitimacy, so that the control it purports to exercise over its territory and people or its ability to engage in either public or private international transactions is denied. This can lead to governmental contacts with rival groups in the offending state and de facto recognition of their right to govern. Of course, derecognition of one government can result in de jure recognition of a rival government.

The United States on many occasions has severed diplomatic relations with governments it found unacceptable for ideological reasons or because of the government's aggressive conduct. Examples include the three Axis governments at the beginning of U.S. military involvement in World War II, the Castro regime in Cuba, Iran in 1979, and Iraq in 1990. U.S. derecognition of the Republic of China occurred in 1979, when the United States recognized the People's Republic of China. But the United States has maintained de facto relations with the government on Taiwan since then.[19] At other times, as in Libya in 1979, the United States may not formally break diplomatic ties, but may close its embassy or reduce its relations to the lowest operational level.

Termination of diplomatic relations may be an appropriate weapon in some self-determination situations. The offending government may be either a parent government acting against a self-determination movement or a new government violating international law or the conditions it accepted for recognition during its formation. Derecognition may be more symbolic than effective, however, in changing governmental behavior. Moreover, derecognition may do more harm than good by alienating the offending government—thus making it even more insecure and belligerent—and removing

---

[18]Here we use the term "derecognition" loosely to signify at a minimum a termination of diplomatic relations.

[19]See David J. Scheffer, "The Law of Treaty Termination as Applied to the United States De-Recognition of the Republic of China," *Harvard International Law Journal*, vol. 19 (Fall 1978), pp. 944–61.

vital channels of communication with and persuasion from the outside world. But derecognition may also leave some diplomatic channels open and thus serve as a useful and highly symbolic punitive act without completely isolating the offending government.

Expelling or suspending the offending government from international and regional organizations is another delegitimizing and sometimes complementary action. In 1956, the U.N. General Assembly barred Francisco Franco's Spain from membership in U.N. agencies and recommended that all U.N. member states immediately recall their ambassadors from Madrid. Also in 1956, the General Assembly refused to accept the credentials of the Hungarian delegation, and in 1972 it rejected the credentials of the South African delegation. The Organization of American States decided in 1962 that the Marxist-Leninist government of Cuba would be excluded from participation in the inter-American system. Beginning in April 1992, the United States actively lobbied to suspend "Yugoslavia" from membership in the CSCE, and later sought its expulsion from the United Nations and other institutions, after it was reduced to the rump state of Serbia and Montenegro and Serbian aggression continued in Bosnia. The U.S. initiative was not easily achieved. Russia, for example, opposed suspending Yugoslavia from the CSCE. There are no CSCE procedures for such a radical step. A compromise finally emerged to suspend Yugoslavia for 90 days beginning with the July 1992 CSCE summit. Problems can arise when the organization is conceived to be universal in its membership, when expulsion procedures in the organization's charter are either cumbersome or nonexistent, or when other members are opposed.[20] Nevertheless, expulsion or the threat of expulsion from multilateral institutions should exert considerable influence on an offending government.

Conditionality and Economic Sanctions

Economic leverage—in the form of conditioning foreign assistance or imposing sanctions—can be one of the most effective means to influence a

---

[20]See D.W. Bowett, *The Law of International Institutions*, 4th ed. (London: Stevens & Sons, 1982), pp. 390–94.

parent government or a new government. It can also lead to great hardship for the people of a country or region.

The tools of economic conditionality and sanctions can be employed when a parent government violates norms of international law regarding a minority, including one striving for self-determination; fails to engage in a reasonable dialogue with a self-determination movement, thus risking a violent upheaval; or comes to power by terminating a democratic government established under international supervision. They also can be wielded when a new government, having pledged to the recognition criteria proposed in Chapter Five or other criteria, intentionally fails to carry through with its pledges.

Economic conditionality refers to the placement of conditions on bilateral foreign aid or multilateral development or financial assistance. The World Bank and the International Monetary Fund condition the granting of aid and loans to their member states. The requirement to develop market-oriented economies and promote democratic institutions will probably figure prominently in assistance to the successor states of the Soviet Union.

The United States doubtless will condition its bilateral foreign assistance to the successor states of the Soviet Union on continued compliance with the U.S. recognition criteria for those states. The U.S. foreign assistance program already includes conditionality on a wide range of issues, such as human rights, communism, and terrorism. A more systematic review of the foreign aid program is required in order to enhance its utility as leverage on uncooperative parent governments and recalcitrant new governments.

Economic sanctions have remained a frequent means of expressing U.S. and international disapproval of governmental conduct during the post–Cold War era.[21] U.N.-imposed economic sanctions against Iraq in 1990 proved that a sanctions regime can be organized and enforced against an aggressor state, even though it did not accomplish its principal purpose of liberating Kuwait.[22] One reason for continuing economic sanctions against Iraq may become the government's treatment of the Kurds and Shia in its population, groups struggling for their human rights and for self-determination

---

[21]In recent years economic sanctions were imposed or continued against the People's Republic of China, Cuba, Iraq, Libya, South Africa, and Vietnam.

[22]See U.N. Sec. Council Res. 661 (XLIV), August 6, 1990, and Sec. Council Res. 665 (XLIV), August 25, 1990.

(not necessarily secession). In May 1992, the United Nations directed member states to cease all economic and financial transactions with Serbia and Montenegro because of Belgrade's role in fueling aggressive Serbian actions within Bosnia-Herzegovina, including the military occupation of most of that state.[23] The United States joined with the Organization of American States to impose stiff economic sanctions on Haiti following the military coup in September 1991.[24]

Economic sanctions have a disturbing aspect that the United States and the world community have yet to fully resolve. They can bring almost unconscionable hardship upon civilian populations, without achieving their political objective. This may have happened in Haiti and in some areas of Iraq. Sanctions can also undermine the efforts of a minority under siege from an aggressive parent or predecessor government if they cut off that group's economic lifeline or access to military armaments for self-defense. There have been complaints to this effect among the Kurds of northern Iraq and among Slavic Muslims in Bosnia.

Economic sanctions need to be examined carefully in terms of their likely influence on governmental behavior and their impact on civilian populations. The timing of economic sanctions is also critical. If the world community waits too long before imposing the sanctions, their influence on the process may be fatally undermined. Part of the problem in Yugoslavia was not imposing serious sanctions soon enough, before passions overwhelmed all consideration of rational self-interest by the Serbian government and armed militia. Instances will surely arise (as the Iraqi, Haitian, and Bosnian experiences suggest) in which economic sanctions will be insufficient to change the course of events, and more forceful means should be applied sooner to avert human catastrophe and widespread destruction of property. Sanctions can sometimes be a convenient way to orchestrate punitive action while avoiding the hard decisions that must be made to end aggression, protect minorities, and bring humanitarian crises to an end. Economic sanctions may prove impractical under dire circumstances that demand timely collective intervention.

---

[23]See U.N. Sec. Council Res. 757 (XLVI), May 30, 1992.

[24]OAS Ministers of Foreign Affairs Resolutions 1/91 (October 3, 1991) and 2/91 (October 8, 1991). Reprinted in *U.S. Department of State Dispatch*, vol. 2 (1991), pp. 760–61. In a controversial move months later, however, the United States eased its own application of the OAS sanctions by permitting American-owned factories in Haiti to re-open and resume trade.

Military Intervention

T he violence associated with the breakup of Yugoslavia, and governmental or anarchic oppression against populations that are deprived of the right of self-determination in places such as Haiti, Myanmar, and Somalia, raise fundamental questions about the need for and the role of military intervention to alleviate mass human suffering and establish just governance in some existing states. There is also a compelling case to be made for the intervention of military forces in a peacekeeping capacity in order to maintain a cease-fire or to raise the risks for a government bent on launching aggressive actions.

Although the circumstances of each conflict will vary, in general the world community needs to act more quickly and with more determination to employ military force when it proves necessary and feasible. Unilateral interventions to support or oppose self-determination movements, however, are not the answer. In most cases, unilateral intervention would violate principles of international law and establish precedents that could only lead to more lawless behavior by governments.

There is a growing realization that if military force is to be used it should be applied collectively—that collective uses of military force can be legitimate means to achieve legitimate ends. Initiatives at the United Nations and in various regional organizations are beginning to move in this direction.[25] We believe that the United States must work with other governments— including those in the developing world—to support the collective use of military force in appropriate circumstances. In stating this we do not underestimate the obstacles, including the reluctance of nations to use force and to pay their share of the cost of peacekeeping operations. But we believe that the need is compelling. The use of collective force should be considered to achieve the following objectives relating to claims of self-determination:

Preventing Armed Conflict. In his report to the Security Council, *An Agenda for Peace,* U.N. secretary-general Boutros Boutros-Ghali proposes "preventive deployment," meaning the deployment of U.N.-authorized forces

---

[25]See Boutros-Ghali, par. 38; David J. Scheffer, "Toward a Modern Doctrine of Humanitarian Intervention," *University of Toledo Law Review*, vol. 23 (Winter 1992), pp. 264–86.

to an area where military conflict threatens in order to deter a potential aggressor.[26] Since many likely military conflicts are and will continue to be linked to self-determination, much could be gained from deploying forces to deter would-be aggressors and encourage peaceful resolution of disputes arising from a self-determination claim before armed combat overtakes the process.

Preventive deployments would not be intended to keep the peace following a cease-fire (the traditional U.N. peacekeeping operation) but to prevent armed conflict from occurring in the first place. The deployed forces may need to be heavily armed and stationed indefinitely. The deterrent value of the preventive deployment will depend in large part on the force's demonstrated willingness to fight if challenged. Thus it will require an explicit mandate to fight and rules of engagement that provide it with sufficient flexibility to engage in combat.

Most such preventive deployments would have to be with the consent of the relevant party or parties. There would be little basis under international law to intervene, even collectively, without consent where no imminent threat to peace and security existed. The real question is who the relevant parties should be to grant consent. If civil war threatens to erupt within a state where a self-determination movement is seeking territorial autonomy or secession, the consent of the central government alone should be sufficient to permit the introduction of a collective military force to act as a buffer between the government and the separatists. This may also be true when a new government of a new state emerging from a self-determination struggle requires military intervention to prevent a minority within the new state from triggering a civil war in its own attempt to secede or gain autonomy.

It will be more difficult, but not impossible, for preventive deployment to proceed at the sole request of a self-determination movement. A request by the Kurds of northern Iraq, for example, for a massive collective intervention to deter the Iraqi army from overwhelming the Kurdish population in an aggressive campaign would, in our opinion, be fully justified. The presence of U.N. guards and the threat of U.S. air power in northern Iraq after the Gulf war served a similar purpose of deterrence and can be regarded as a modest example of collective intervention for preventive purposes.

---

[26]Boutros-Ghali, pars. 28–32.

Another basis for preventive deployment would be to deter external aggression against a new state or government that has emerged from a self-determination claim. In this case, consent only needs to be obtained from the government on whose territory the preventive deployment is to take place. For example, a collective military presence in Bosnia in early 1992 to deter Serbian aggression launched from both within and outside Bosnia would have been justified. The new Bosnian government requested international military assistance in May and June 1992, but no nation (other than Croatia) or international or regional organization heeded its plea until July and August 1992, long after thousands had been killed and hundreds of thousands rendered homeless.[27] International and regional organizations and groups of nations that participate in a preventive deployment must be prepared for those forces to enter combat if armed conflict breaks out between opposing sides in a self-determination bid. Preventive deployment is not a question of troops fighting their way into a conflict that already has erupted into warfare, but of being prepared to respond to aggression if and when it occurs following the preventive deployment. Thus a commitment to preventive deployment can be far-reaching and costly, but it can also achieve its objective of preventing a devastating war.

Delivering Humanitarian Assistance. Perhaps the most frequently invoked purpose for collective military intervention in internal conflicts of all kinds will be to ensure the delivery of humanitarian assistance to civilian populations under siege. When a self-determination claim triggers an armed conflict that becomes a humanitarian crisis, getting food, medicine, and shelter to thousands or millions of civilians becomes an inescapable imperative. A new intolerance for such human tragedies is becoming evident in the post–Cold War world and is redefining the principle of non-interference in the internal affairs of states.[28]

The recent humanitarian crises in northern Iraq, Bosnia, and Somalia, and the varied international responses to them, have established important precedents that will be further developed in the years ahead. As of mid-1992, neither the United States nor the world community has reached a point where

---

[27]See "Bosnia Pleads for Help Against 'Aggression'," *Washington Post*, May 5, 1992, p. A21; "Bosnian, Desperate Over Shelling, Appeals to U.S. for an Air Attack," *New York Times*, June 9, 1992, p. A1.

[28]Scheffer, "Humanitarian Intervention," pp. 253–93.

humanitarian calamities resulting from self-determination claims or internal repression automatically trigger collective military intervention to accomplish strictly humanitarian objectives. But humanitarian interventions will become increasingly unavoidable.

The purpose of collective military intervention for humanitarian purposes is not necessarily to engage in combat but rather to provide adequate military protection for humanitarian relief workers to do their job of delivering the aid directly to the individuals who need it. The show of force should help deter attacks on relief convoys, airlifts, and humanitarian personnel. But the intervention also must be planned and deployed with the capability of using force to repel attacks and clear corridors for delivery of relief supplies if necessary.

In the future, the United States and other countries will need to respond to humanitarian crises with more backbone than they evidenced in the case of Bosnia or Somalia by mid-1992. The United States was not alone in its tardy response to these events. The European Community avoided intervention. U.S. pressure on the European Community in May 1992 helped to spur more definitive action in response to the plight of the Bosnians. The Community imposed trade sanctions on Serbia and Montenegro in May 1992, and the U.N. Security Council soon followed with its own economic sanctions against Serbia and Montenegro. But policymakers in Washington, London, Paris, Berlin, and other capitals feared the loss of their own soldiers' lives in the "quagmire" of Bosnia. The fact that the conflict initially appears strictly internal should not bar collective military intervention to ensure that civilians receive humanitarian aid.[29]

In December 1991, the U.N. General Assembly adopted a resolution reorganizing its humanitarian relief operations.[30] While the United Nations now possesses additional authority and capabilities to respond to humanitarian emergencies, the General Assembly balked at forcing a government to accept humanitarian relief against its will.[31] But where the humanitarian crisis threatens international peace and security—as it almost always

---

[29]See U.N. Sec. Council Res. 757 (XLVI), May 30, 1992. On August 13, 1992, the Security Council authorized the use of force to deliver humanitarian aid in Bosnia. See "U.N. Council Votes for Use of Force for Bosnia Relief," *New York Times*, August 14, 1992, p. A1.

[30]U.N.G.A. Res. 46/182 (XLVI), December 17, 1991.

[31]Scheffer, "Humanitarian Intervention," pp. 280–82. In many cases, however, there will be no effective governing authority, or the self-determination movement may be the de facto governing body in the territory.

will—the U.N. Security Council can and should act more affirmatively to deliver assistance to victims within a state.

It will sometimes prove impossible to separate the humanitarian from the political objectives of a collective military intervention. The only way to ensure continued access to humanitarian relief may be to directly engage aggressive forces, thereby bringing about a cessation of the hostilities and thus an advantage to either the central government or the self-determination movement. International and regional security organizations and the United States should not shrink from this responsibility. A leading priority must be the survival of innocent civilians, including those struggling for self-determination.

Defending a New State. The easiest case to make for collective military intervention in response to self-determination is to defend a new state from external aggression, including militia operating internally but supported by a foreign government. Principles of collective self-defense would provide traditional justification for such intervention, but these principles have not been implemented in recent times. New states have emerged from the trials of self-determination only to stand exposed to massive foreign military intervention and occupation. Serbian aggression and occupation in Croatia and Bosnia is the starkest example of this. Many successor states to the Soviet Union fear Russian armed intervention to occupy lands inhabited by Russian minorities.

The U.N. Security Council should be better prepared to identify aggression when it occurs either internally or across international borders and to authorize collective military action to defend the territorial integrity of a new state, including the recapture of lands seized by a foreign aggressor or a foreign-backed militia. Prior to Security Council action, individual nations can respond to appeals for aid from a beleaguered state under the principle of collective self-defense and through regional arrangements.[32] The United States, which in recent years often trumpeted the principle of collective self-defense to justify its own military actions overseas,[33] must recognize that self-defense principles also apply to newly created states. Otherwise, the principle of self-determination that underpins the new state will

---

[32]See U.N. Charter, Articles 51-54.

[33]See, for example, Abraham D. Sofaer, "International Law and the Use of Force," *The National Interest*, no. 13 (Fall 1988), pp. 53–64.

be fatally undermined by a failure to uphold that state's territorial integrity and political independence.[34]

Advancing the Cause of Self-Determination. An exception to the principle of non-use of force seemed to take hold during the Cold War, namely that foreign military intervention could be justified to liberate a people and their colony or state from alien or colonial domination.[35] Anti-colonial self-determination, however, has largely passed into history. Today only a limited number of circumstances justify collective military intervention to advance a self-determination claim. First, the self-determination movement should meet the criteria set forth in Chapter Five. Second, the self-determination movement's very existence would have to be imperiled by an oppressive and aggressive central government and military; indicators of this would be violations on a massive scale of the group's minority rights. Third, initiatives to settle peacefully the dispute between the parent government and the self-determination movement must be exhausted. Even then, the need for a collective military intervention to save lives and preserve the rights of the minority must be unambiguous. The use of military force to create a new state would require conduct by the parent government so egregious that it has forfeited any right to govern the minority claiming self-determination.

Guaranteeing Compliance with Recognition Criteria. Chapter Five discussed the need for a new government to commit to an enforcement mechanism that would guarantee compliance with the recognition criteria before the United States extends formal diplomatic ties. Through this mechanism, the new government consents in advance to a collective intervention to influence its own compliance if it seriously violates the criteria pertaining to the inviolability of borders, the non-use of force, or a limited constitutional democracy including protection of minority rights. The prior consent by the government permitting such action means that the principle of non-interference in the internal affairs of states is not violated. The new government's prior consent may not hold up under the pressures of an actual crisis or a difference of opinion between the new government and the relevant

---

[34]The fate of Bosnia-Herzegovina following Serbian aggression and occupation in 1992 offers a stark example.

[35]See W. Michael Reisman, "Allocating Competences to Use Coercion in the Post–Cold War World: Practices, Conditions, and Prospects," in *Law and Force in the New International Order*, ed. Lori Fisler Damrosch and David J. Scheffer (Boulder: Westview Press, 1991), pp. 29–34.

collective body. But at a minimum, prior consent provides a basis upon which to organize collective action against the offending government. Because implementation of the enforcement mechanism in any particular instance requires explicit authorization by the U.N. Security Council or a regional organization, military intervention in this circumstance, like in others, requires collective approval.

Defending the Central Government. Throughout the Cold War the United States often defended governments against even large segments of their own people. Today, however, military intervention to defend a central government from a self-determination movement can be justified only under limited circumstances. If the central government is not oppressing the minority group and giving it cause to take up arms against its authority, and if the insurgency itself is not acting on behalf of a legitimate self-determination claim that has no alternative but to resort to force because of the government's conduct, a basis might be found to defend the legitimately constituted government of the country. This may not require collective intervention if a unilateral intervention is justifiable as an act of collective self-defense of a legitimate government; U.S. military assistance to the Philippine government to fight communist insurgents on various islands of the country is an example. Once an internal conflict has become a full-fledged civil war, however, other considerations, including humanitarian, predominate and justification for collective military intervention becomes the critical issue.

In presenting this range of situations for collective military intervention, we are not suggesting that the decision to use collective military force be made lightly. There is strong resistance to military intervention, much of it for very good reasons. We are not advocating the repeal of those provisions of the U.N. Charter that prohibit the threat or use of force against the territorial integrity or political independence of any U.N. member (Article 2(4)) or interference in a member's internal affairs (Article 2(7)). We acknowledge and have great sympathy for the arguments counseling against committing American and other military forces to combat. However, when American interests in the new world order, including the humanitarian imperatives of so many distant conflicts, demand international or regional action, the U.S. government (led by a determined president) should use its leverage as a superpower to forge the necessary domestic and international consensus to respond.

Three Proposals for Institutional Reform

he task of managing self-determination in the new world order requires a fundamental reassessment of the capabilities of international institutions and of the United States to organize effectively for the challenges of the new era. Can the United Nations, for example, adapt quickly enough to shepherd peaceful means of managing self-determination and to respond effectively with collective military force to the armed conflicts that will continue to erupt in connection with self-determination claims? We propose three institutional initiatives that would address this question. The first is to use the United Nations more effectively to manage self-determination movements, the second is to create a standby military force for deployment by the U.N. Security Council, and the third focuses on the organization of the U.S. government.

U.N. Oversight

The United Nations has the capabilities and organizational structure to quickly establish a more comprehensive oversight capability for self-determination movements. The United Nations also needs a mechanism that can deal with self-determination movements and the conflicts they spawn more efficiently and comprehensively than is now the case. There are two possible approaches (not necessarily incompatible with each other) that would not require amending the U.N. Charter.

The first approach would be to create a special committee in the Security Council that would include not only the members of the Council but also Germany and Japan as well as other major regional powers (perhaps two from each region).[36] The committee would be authorized by the Security Council to monitor self-determination movements and to alert the Council whenever a situation appeared likely to escalate into a threat to the peace. Alternatively, the Security Council could appoint the U.N. Trusteeship Council as its adviser on self-determination issues. These are modest but realistic proposals that focus on the security implications of self-determination movements.

---

[36]Article 29 of the U.N. Charter empowers the Security Council to "establish such subsidiary organs as it deems necessary for the performance of its function."

The second approach would be to transform the near-moribund Trusteeship Council into a modern international clearinghouse for self-determination.[37] These movements need a forum in which to lodge their claims, identify and understand their rights, negotiate with government authorities, establish just administration of their affairs, and peacefully work out realistic political and territorial arrangements for the future.

The trusteeship system is one of the lesser known success stories of the United Nations. All but one of the former trust territories achieved independence or merged with adjoining states. When the island of Palau in the Pacific Ocean finally irons out its relationship with the United States, the original trusteeship system will expire for lack of clients.

The membership of the Trusteeship Council—which operates under the authority of the General Assembly—includes the five permanent members of the Security Council, any U.N. members administering trust territories, and a limited number of other U.N. members. The objectives of the new trusteeship system would remain as stated in the Charter—to further international peace and security, to promote progressive development toward self-government or independence, to encourage respect for human rights and fundamental freedoms, and to ensure equal treatment in social, economic, and commercial matters for U.N. member states and their nationals.[38]

Under the modern system, the "trust territory" would be that part of a member state voluntarily placed into trusteeship by the government of that state for the purpose of resolving a self-determination claim under U.N. supervision.[39] The Charter provides that the administering authority of the trust territory "may be one or more states or the Organization itself."[40] Thus the United Nations acting through the Trusteeship Council could administer the trust territory in the manner agreed upon by the concerned parties, including the ruling government. A trusteeship agreement would lock in the cooperation or acquiescence of the ruling government.

---

[37]Chapters XII and XIII of the U.N. Charter embody the constitutional authority to accomplish this. See David J. Scheffer, "How the UN Can Deal With the Dangerous Pieces," *International Herald Tribune*, January 31, 1992, p. 6.

[38]See U.N. Charter, Article 76.

[39]This admittedly would require a narrow reading of U.N. Charter Article 78, which states, "The trusteeship system shall not apply to territories which have become Members of the United Nations." This provision might eliminate from a modern trusteeship system the small group of independent states that previously were U.N. trust territories.

[40]U.N. Charter, Article 81.

At first blush, this may seem implausible. What government, after all, would forfeit its sovereign power over any of its territory? But designation of a new trust territory would not predetermine any particular governmental arrangement for the region and its people in the future. Depending on how negotiations and planning proceed under Trusteeship Council oversight, the trust territory might be re-absorbed as a fully integral part of the existing state; it might become an autonomous entity within the state; it might become an independent state or merge with a neighboring state. For central governments under political siege or embroiled in bloody civil wars, the Trusteeship Council would be a way out of a seemingly unsolvable dilemma. There would be a procedure and a means by which to address a self-determination claim. The trusteeship system could save untold numbers of lives from humanitarian crises and avoid the devastation of civil war—tragedies that ultimately can imperil the very existence of a ruling government.

Some new trust territories could be designated "strategic areas" under the Charter because of their threat of civil war.[41] They would then fall under the direct jurisdiction of the Security Council, which could deploy U.N. peacekeeping forces or impose sanctions to prevent armed conflict. If, under the first approach, a special committee were established by the Security Council to monitor and advise on self-determination movements, then it could coordinate directly with the Trusteeship Council.

The Trusteeship Council also could work with member states to develop the criteria for recognition of new states that might emerge from trust territories and to establish with greater clarity and detail the conditions for admission to the United Nations set forth in Article 4(1) of the Charter.

Modernizing the U.N. Trusteeship Council would require considerable preparatory work on the part of the United Nations and, in particular, the permanent members of the Security Council. We do not underestimate the difficulties. But the current ad hoc manner in which self-determination is being addressed by the United Nations and other institutions urgently requires a more systematic process. If the international trusteeship system is not restored and modernized, some other mechanism will need to be devised.

---

[41]U.N. Charter, Articles 82 and 83.

U.N. Military Enforcement Capability

This chapter has discussed the need and justification for collective military intervention. Fortunately, the means to create and deploy, quickly and frequently if necessary, a multinational force acting under the authority of the U.N. Security Council already exists, although it has never been implemented.

Article 43 of the U.N. Charter established the legal basis for a U.N. enforcement capability.[42] In 1945, the drafters of the Charter (as well as the U.S. Congress) intended to provide the Security Council with forces drawn from the national contingents of member states (starting with the five permanent members of the Council) that would be available "on call" on a case-by-case basis to enforce Security Council resolutions under Article 42 of the Charter.[43] The particular mix of national contingents for any particular action would vary depending upon the military needs and political sensitivities involved in each case. For example, the Security Council may determine that U.S. forces should not be deployed in a particular conflict, but that U.S. communications and intelligence support should be provided.

The framers of the Charter did not intend to create a permanent U.N. army. Member states were to have entered into "special" agreements with the Security Council that would stipulate in sufficient detail the rights and responsibilities of the contributing state and the limits of U.N. authority—including command authority—over the forces dedicated to U.N. service. While the Military Staff Committee described in Chapter VII of the Charter would help draw up plans for the application of armed force and be responsible for the "strategic direction of any armed forces placed at the

---

[42]Article 43 of the U.N. Charter states:
  1. All Members of the United Nations, in order to contribute to the maintenance of international peace and security, undertake to make available to the Security Council, on its call and in accordance with a special agreement or agreements, armed forces, assistance, and facilities, including rights of passage, necessary for the purpose of maintaining international peace and security.
  2. Such agreement or agreements shall govern the numbers and types of forces, their degree of readiness and general location, and the nature of the facilities and assistance to be provided.
  3. The agreement or agreements shall be negotiated as soon as possible on the initiative of the Security Council. They shall be concluded between the Security Council and Members or between the Security Council and groups of Members and shall be subject to ratification by the signatory states in accordance with their respective constitutional processes.
[43]See Hans Kelsen, *The Law of the United Nations* (New York: Praeger, 1950), pp. 744–61.

disposal of the Security Council," its functions were to be designated by the Security Council. The Charter explicitly states that, "Questions relating to the command of such forces shall be worked out subsequently."[44] This leaves considerable flexibility for the Security Council, where the United States holds the veto power, to tailor command requirements to the action at hand.

Many issues associated with creating an Article 43 capability were negotiated in 1946 and 1947 by the Military Staff Committee and the Security Council. A model special agreement was drafted in detail, albeit with some disagreement among Security Council members over various provisions.[45] In retrospect, it is remarkable how much agreement was achieved on the eve of the Cold War and how the remaining disagreements should be resolvable now that the United States and Russia are cooperating on so many fronts, including peacekeeping.

In his report to the Security Council, *An Agenda for Peace*, U.N. secretary-general Boutros Boutros-Ghali recommended that Article 43 finally be implemented.[46] This is particularly critical if collective military force is to be used to stop internal armed conflicts associated with self-determination claims. The U.S. Congress planned for a strong U.S. role when it approved the U.N. Participation Act of 1945.[47] Section 6 of that law empowers the president to negotiate an Article 43 special agreement with the Security Council. Both houses of Congress will have to approve the terms of the special agreement. But once the special agreement is adopted, it would commit a designated number of U.S. armed forces to the service of the Security Council on a case-by-case basis. The special agreement could require that operational command of U.S. forces always remain with a U.S. commander.

Other governments also will have to enter into special agreements with the Security Council before a collective force can exist and be operational

---

[44]U.N. Charter, Article 47(3).

[45]See United Nations, *Repertory of United Nations Practice*, vol. 2, *Articles 23-54 of the Charter* (New York: United Nations, 1955), pp. 393–408. For discussion, see Bowett, *United Nations Forces*, pp. 12–18.

[46]Boutros-Ghali, pars. 42–43.

[47]Public Law 79-264, 59 Stat. 619, approved December 20, 1945. See David J. Scheffer, "War Powers and the U.N. Charter: Constraints on the President's Power to Commit U.S. Armed Forces to Combat Under the Authority of the U.N. Security Council," in "The Constitutional Roles of Congress and the President in Declaring and Waging War," *Hearing of the Senate Judiciary Committee*, 102d Cong., 1st sess., January 8, 1991, pp. 5–27.

for assignment by the Security Council under Chapter VII of the Charter. But a beginning must be made soon before the conflicts erupting in the post–Cold War era overwhelm our capacity to respond and to save lives.

Reorganization of the U.S. Government

As presently organized and staffed, the State Department, Defense Department, and National Security Council still reflect the concerns and priorities of the Cold War. We question whether they would be fully equipped to coordinate and implement on a daily basis this wide range of responses to the difficult challenges that claims of self-determination can now pose. The various responses examined in this book require bilateral, regional, and international policies and strategies. These responses often will overlap, with monitoring and economic sanctions being applied one day, and a collective military intervention being launched the next.

The consequences of implementing any particular response may impair other foreign or domestic policies. More thought must, therefore, be given to the proper organization of the U.S. government to undertake these new foreign policy agendas, such as proliferating self-determination movements and the internal conflicts that are erupting across the globe. While we have proposed that the U.N. Trusteeship Council might be an appropriate international forum for a more comprehensive and coordinated response to modern developments in self-determination, we have not proposed any specific re-organization of the federal bureaucracy or the creation of any new agency. Such tasks are beyond the scope of this study. We do propose, however, that serious consideration be given to how the U.S. government is organized and staffed to respond efficiently and wisely to the volatile character of modern self-determination.

CONCLUSION

In this volume, we have sought to answer the fundamental question of how demands for self-determination should be managed in a turbulent new world. The pressures for self-determination in many parts of the world have been suppressed for decades by dictatorships of the right and left. The collapse of communism and the growing worldwide pressure for democracy are unleashing movements with broad public support. The number and variety of self-determination movements thus are growing, as bewildered governments and multilateral institutions try to understand them and decide how to respond. Internal ethnic conflicts are proliferating, compelling national and international responses before considered policies can be developed. The challenge for the United States and the world community is to respond to the breakup of some nations and the restoration of others in ways that minimize violence and human suffering and maximize the chances for establishing democratic governments.

The old assumption that the boundaries set after World War II were permanent has been shaken by events in the Soviet Union and Yugoslavia. However, as we have tried to demonstrate, the United States and the world community continue to be shackled by the instinct that existing states and governments should be supported at almost any cost in their efforts to preserve the status quo.

Because we believe that greater analytic clarity will help with the management of specific situations, we have introduced several new terms to describe as pragmatically as possible how self-determination is manifesting itself in the new world order. For example, "sub-state self-determination" describes a prominent development in many countries that is not necessarily ethnic in character or separatist in design. The categories of self-determination described in Chapter Three should help policymakers and others clarify and better respond to such claims.

A clearer understanding of the variety of self-determination movements must be followed by the adoption of standards and criteria for evaluating each situation. In responding to events in the Soviet Union and Yugoslavia, the U.S. government developed new criteria for recognition of successor states, focusing as much on the internal characteristics of states as on their agreement to accept the basic norms of international conduct. All of this is to be applauded.

However, although bold conditions for U.S. recognition were imposed upon the successor states of the Soviet Union, they were hurriedly signed off on in an attempt to reduce the danger of nuclear proliferation and to contain Islamic expansionism in Central Asia. In Yugoslavia, U.S. policy remained focused on preserving Yugoslavia as a state while the European Community took the lead in recognizing the new states of Slovenia and Croatia.

The United States and the world community must not wait to address self-determination claims until after a ruling government has collapsed or armed conflict has erupted. Rather the international community—including governments and multilateral institutions—must be involved early in the process to seek to satisfy the demands of self-determination short of creating a new state. This requires, among other things, accurately identifying the claim, examining the conduct of both the ruling government and the self-determination movement, considering historical factors, seeking to judge the will of the people, and taking account of potentially violent consequences.

In most instances, U.S. policy should encourage the preservation of an existing state, particularly when the self-determination movement itself does not seek separate statehood. In these situations, the protection of minority rights within the existing state will demand a bolder and more principled U.S. policy that encourages a more representative government as well as a more sympathetic response to the self-determination claim. In other cases, however, the United States will need to deal forthrightly with the issue of secession as some self-determination movements press their claims for independence.

The principles discussed in Chapter Five are intended to influence how new states are created and how new governments conduct both domestic and foreign affairs following independence. Some of the conditions mirror what binds or should bind all states, such as obligations under the U.N. Charter, respect for international law, the inviolability of borders, a commitment to resolving disputes peacefully, and protection of individual and minority rights. Other conditions are more intrusive and uniquely tailored for newly emerging states: adherence to certain arms control treaties, the creation of a constitutional democracy including the holding of free elections, the right of political dissent, limits on arbitrary police power, an enforcement mechanism to guarantee compliance, and moves toward a market-oriented economy if the new state hopes to receive foreign assistance.

The process of self-determination and of new governments being held accountable to recognition criteria can break down, necessitating a wide range of diplomatic, economic, and military interventions in response to self-determination claims that come under siege or to noncompliance by a new government. These actions include monitoring human rights, minority rights, and other activities within states where self-determination has taken hold; applying diplomatic pressure on recalcitrant parties; denying a government—the parent government or a newly-constituted government—international legitimacy because of its conduct in relation to self-determination issues; and conditioning foreign assistance and imposing economic sanctions on a government that violates accepted norms of behavior.

Collective military intervention must be available as a response in some situations, such as preventing armed conflict, delivering humanitarian assistance, defending a new state, advancing the cause of self-determination in certain limited circumstances, occasionally guaranteeing compliance with the recognition criteria, and in some cases defending an existing government from limited insurgencies. The American people, however, are reluctant to take on new international responsibilities. They resist new commitments that will drain resources from domestic needs and that could involve the United States in a new quagmire. In warning that Yugoslavia could become another Lebanon or Vietnam, the Bush administration was evoking images with strong resonance among Americans.

We do not underestimate the difficulties of overcoming these popular instincts. At the same time, the tragic events in the former state of Yugoslavia during 1991 and 1992 are a harbinger of what the pressures for self-determination are capable of bringing in the future unless the United States and the world community alter their approach to such movements.

An approach that emphasizes early policymaking and a more engaged relationship with self-determination movements should improve opportunities to achieve peaceful and more lasting resolutions to these seemingly intractable problems. The United States must begin the long but necessary task of build-ing a consensus among other governments about the principles to apply and the actions needed in particular situations. At the same time, the United States needs to recognize that some countries view the new U.S. interest in democracy and self-determination as yet another pretext for U.S. inter-vention in the internal affairs of other states in support of U.S. security and economic interests. These objections no doubt will persist, but the United States can blunt them by avoiding double standards in the application of the principles and engaging in coercive intervention only with the support of the international community.

New norms of international law will need to be developed and agree-ment among governments sought in order to provide a principled basis for a more activist and comprehensive response to self-determination claims, many of which can trigger armed conflict and human misery. That process has begun. We must also understand the new and diverse character of self-determination claims. We need to forge relationships between governments and peoples that foster the peaceful accommodation of popular aspirations for more responsive, representative government. The principles set forth in this book offer a conceptual framework for these necessary endeavors.

APPENDIX

GLOBAL SURVEY OF SELF-DETERMINATION MOVEMENTS

AFRICA

ANGOLA

sub-state

Cabinda

• A region geographically separate from but administered by Angola, Cabinda was plagued by intensifying secessionist violence as Angola's September 1992 national elections approached. Cabinda's feeling of distinctiveness from Angola is deeply rooted, because most of its 100,000 residents belong to an ethnic group linked to the population of southwestern Zaire. The Angolan government has stationed 15,000 troops in the region to control the situation.

BURKINA FASO

representative

• Since gaining independence from France in 1960, Burkina Faso has been ruled by a series of military governments. A constitution outlining a multiparty system was approved by the legislature in December 1990 and backed by 93 percent of voters in June 1991. However, when Burkina Faso's president refused to schedule a national conference on the transition to democracy, opposition groups staged protests that brought violent clashes with government supporters. All candidates

Note: This survey, current as of mid-1992, is not comprehensive, but attempts to cover a broad geographical range and the full spectrum of claim types. The inclusion or exclusion of a particular movement does not reflect a judgment on the merits of its claim.

challenging the president in December 1991 elections withdrew from the race in protest of the refusal to schedule the conference.

BURUNDI

representative

• Burundi remains a one-party state. In 1991 voters endorsed a National Unity Charter designed to further democracy and to ease ethnic tensions. Burundi has historically been plagued by ethnic violence between the majority Hutus and the minority Tutsi, who control the government; a number of Hutu political movements of varying militancy exist. In August 1988, ethnic violence killed thousands (mostly Hutus) in Burundi's northern provinces.

CAMEROON

representative

• Although opposition parties were legalized in Cameroon in December 1990, power remains concentrated in a single party. Government resistance to opposition demands that a national conference be called and a new constitution developed led to anti-government demonstrations in April 1991. The government responded with a violent crackdown, placing seven of its ten provinces under military rule in May 1991. Cameroon held its first full parliamentary elections in March 1992, although they were boycotted by three opposition parties.

sub-state

• The Republic of Cameroon was formed in 1961 by the union of former French and British colonial possessions. The French portion gained independence in 1960. In 1961, a plebiscite was administered separately in the northern and southern portions of the British territories, which were to choose between independence through federation with Nigeria and independence through federation with French Cameroun. The southern portion chose the latter and a loose federal structure was formed. That structure evolved into a centralized regime between 1965 and 1972. As a result, tensions between the 25 percent Anglophone minority and the French-speaking majority persist. The Cameroon Anglophone Movement seeks full independence for the former British portion, charging that the declaration of a unitary state in 1972 abrogated the agreement under which the former French and British territories were joined.

CHAD

representative

- In December 1990, Chad's President Hissen Habré was overthrown by Colonel Idris Deby, who promised multiparty reforms and presidential elections. In May 1991, Deby responded to opposition parties' demands with assurances that he would hold a national conference to draft a new constitution. As of mid-1992, the conference had not yet been convened, with ethnic divisions continuing to hamper the government.

DJIBOUTI

representative / sub-state

- Tensions between members of the ruling Issa tribe and the Afar tribe escalated into open military confrontation in northern Djibouti in November and December 1991. The Afars, organized into the Revolutionary Front for the Restoration of Unity and Democracy, demanded a greater role in running the country and a multiparty democracy. Djibouti's president has promised to hold a referendum on multiparty democracy.

ETHIOPIA

representative

- The government of Colonel Mengistu Haile Mariam faced a number of rebellions throughout his 17-year rule, which began in 1974. In 1975, the Marxist-Leninist Tigrean People's Liberation Front (TPLF) launched a campaign to oust Mengistu. In 1988, the TPLF formed a broader coalition movement, the Ethiopian People's Revolutionary Democratic Front (EPRDF), for the same purpose. Along with the Eritrean People's Liberation Front and the Oromo Liberation Front (OLF), the EPRDF launched a decisive offensive against the Mengistu government in February 1991. Mengistu fled the country in May 1991, and a coalition government took control, with the EPRDF and the OLF the main partners. The OLF withdrew from the coalition and boycotted Ethiopia's elections in June 1992.

sub-state

Eritrea

- Unlike the rest of Ethiopia, Eritrea was colonized by Italy during the late nineteenth century. After World War II, Eritrea was administered by Britain until it was federated with Ethiopia as an autonomous unit in 1952. Despite the region's autonomous status, Eritrea's trade unions and pro-independence parties were banned. Eritrean forces began an armed drive for secession in 1961; the region was formally stripped of its autonomous status in 1962. After a 30-year civil war involving 500,000 deaths, Eritrean forces, in conjunction with other rebel groups, defeated the Ethiopian army in May 1991. Leaders established a provisional government in the province and agreed to submit the question of independence to an open referendum, subject to international oversight, in mid-1993. Eritrea exists as a de facto state, with separate immigration procedures and a different exchange rate.

• A number of groups in several regions of Ethiopia continue to call for autonomy or independence. The largest of Ethiopia's ethnic groups, the Oromo, accounts for between 45 and 60 percent of the population and numbers more than 22 million people. The Oromo language and culture have been banned since the 1950s. The OLF, which allied with the EPRDF in defeating the Mengistu government but subsequently withdrew from the transitional government, has long sought an independent Islamic state of Oromia in the south. Eight armed groups—the OLF among them—claim control over territory in the eastern Haberge region. Elsewhere, Afar guerrillas have clashed with government forces and are demanding regional autonomy from both the Ethiopian government and the Eritrean provisional government.

KENYA

representative

• Until December 1991, when opposition parties were legalized in Kenya, the Kenyan government had resisted any move toward a multiparty democracy. Western governments suspended aid to Kenya in November 1991 pending political reform. The government continues to argue that a multiparty system would fragment society along ethnic lines. Between October 1991 and mid-1992, ethnic clashes killed about 1,000 people and left 50,000 homeless. The clashes led opponents of the government, including the Catholic Church, to accuse the government of fomenting ethnic conflict to discredit a multiparty system.

MALAWI

representative

• Malawi remains a one-party state ruled by its president-for-life, Hastings Kamuzu Banda. Any political activity outside the ruling Malawi Congress Party is forbidden; groups pressuring for reforms have faced a government crackdown. When the country's Catholic bishops criticized the government in March 1992, the government ordered (although it did not carry out) their execution. In May 1992, government troops fired point-blank upon protesters, killing 38 people. Shortly thereafter, the World Bank and Western donor nations suspended new aid to the government.

MALI

representative

• In March 1991, after three months of pro-democracy marches and demonstrations brought the deaths of approximately 150 civilians, Mali's military ruler was overthrown by soldiers within his army. The military council established to govern the country dissolved itself within a week and turned power over to a transitional government made up of military and civilian members. A multiparty conference in July 1991 developed a new constitution, which was approved in a national referendum in December 1991.

sub-state

• A rebellion of the Tuareg ethnic minority, which demands sovereignty over tracts of land in northern Mali, broke out in summer 1990. A January 1991 agreement to grant autonomy to the Tuaregs in the region they inhabit was ultimately rejected by the rebels when implementation of autonomy was delayed. The Malian military has reportedly engaged in extrajudicial executions and detention of Tuaregs accused of complicity in separatist acts.

MOROCCO

sub-state

Western Sahara

• The sovereignty of Western Sahara has been in dispute since Spain's 1976 withdrawal from the territory. After a 1975 treaty divided the territory between Morocco and Mauritania, the Polisario Front, a liberation movement backed by Libya and Algeria, launched an armed struggle against both Morocco and Mauritania. The Polisario Front proclaimed an independent Saharan Arab Democratic Republic in 1976. Mauritania withdrew its troops in 1979, but the territory vacated by Mauritania has since been contested between Morocco and the Polisario Front. The Saharan Arab Democratic Republic was admitted to the Organization of African Unity (OAU) and recognized by 70 governments. On April 15, 1991, the United Nations adopted a peace plan for the region, calling for a cease-fire and a referendum that would permit people in the Western Sahara to vote for independence or continued affiliation with Morocco. The cease-fire went into effect in September 1991, with a 375-member U.N. peacekeeping force taking up positions soon after. The referendum, scheduled for January 1992, was delayed by the issue of whether only those who resided in the Western Sahara before 1974 should be permitted to vote, or whether later migrants from Morocco should be included.

NIGERIA

representative

• Nigeria's military government has undertaken a tightly-controlled transition designed to turn power over to civilians by January 1993. Authorities legalized two political parties in 1989 and have outlawed the formation of political groupings along ethnic or religious lines. Local elections were held in 1991 and national elections in 1992. Throughout the process, however, the country continued to be plagued by violence between the less populous and wealthier Christians of the south and the poorer but politically dominant Muslims of the north. Outbreaks of Christian-Muslim violence in May 1992 led to approximately 500 deaths. With 250 ethnic groups, Nigeria has seen frequent ethnic violence. The largest recent outbreak of civil strife occurred in the central-eastern state of Taraba, leading to as many as 5,000 deaths between October 1991 and mid-1992.

RWANDA

representative

• Rwanda, long dominated by one party, moved toward a multiparty system with the adoption of a new constitution in mid-1991. In March 1992, opposition leaders and the government agreed to form a transitional government. Throughout the democratization process, however, Rwanda has been plagued by civil strife. A civil war began in October 1990, when more than 1,000 Rwandan refugees invaded the country from neighboring Uganda. The force was largely made up of members of the minority Tutsi tribe, who resent domination by Hutu-led governments. Since 1963, when a country-wide blood-letting precipitated the flight of thousands of Tutsis from the country, communal killings have led to tens of thousands of deaths. In July 1992, government and rebel forces reached agreement on a cease-fire to be monitored by a multinational African military observer team.

SENEGAL

sub-state

Casamance

• The Casamance Democratic Forces Movement has sought the independence of the southern province of Casamance from Senegal since 1982. Casamance has a population of 400,000, a majority of whom are members of the mainly Catholic Diola tribe. Catholics make up only five percent of the overall population in Senegal and resent Muslim domination. The government's counter-insurgency campaign has led thousands of citizens to flee to Guinea-Bissau and the Gambia.

SOMALIA

representative/sub-state

• Somalia was formed in 1960 by union between British Somaliland in the north and Italian Somaliland in the south. Inhabitants of the north, dominated by the Isaak clan (one of six clan families in Somalia) claim that they are discriminated against by the Hawiye and Darod tribes of the south. The Isaak-dominated Somali National Movement began an armed insurgency against the government in 1988. Isaaks have declared an independent country of Somaliland in the north and promised democratic multiparty elections by 1993. Meanwhile, chaos reigns in the south, where sub-clans of the Hawiye clan have been fighting each other in the capital city of Mogadishu since the January 1991 departure of president Mohammed Siad Barre, who had ruled as a dictator for 22 years. The conflict escalated into a full-scale civil war in November 1991. As of mid-1992, tens of thousands had died and an estimated 4.5 million were under threat of starvation.

SOUTH AFRICA

representative

• South Africa's political and social system is based on a policy of racial segregation, or apartheid, under which its 69 percent black majority is not permitted to vote. Unrest among blacks in the country began in 1984 with the promulgation of a constitution denying them representation. Moves toward negotiations on the country's system began in 1989 with the election of F.W. de Klerk as president by white voters. In February 1990, the country began its process of political reform, as President de Klerk announced the release of African National Congress leader Nelson Mandela, who had been imprisoned for 28 years;

unbanned the ANC as well as other anti-apartheid organizations; and paved the way for power-sharing talks as part of a constitutional reform process. Agreement on a multiparty conference to resolve obstacles was reached in early 1991, with the first round of the conference, known as the Convention for a Democratic South Africa (Codesa), taking place in December 1991. In a whites-only referendum in March 1992, 70 percent of voters backed the reform process. In mid-1992, however, continuing violence among blacks prompted the ANC to withdraw from constitutional talks and threatened to undermine prospects for building a multiparty democracy in South Africa.

SUDAN

representative / sub-state

• For 25 of its 35 years of independence, Sudan has been gripped with civil war. Since 1983, the Sudan People's Liberation Army (SPLA), made up of African-Christian southerners, has been fighting against a government historically dominated by Muslim, Arabic-speaking northerners. The SPLA seeks to replace the existing government, establish greater autonomy for the south, and abolish the universal application of Islamic law. In July 1992, after a three-month offensive, government forces captured the SPLA's headquarters in southeastern Sudan.

TANZANIA

sub-state

Zanzibar

• The state of Tanzania was formed in 1964 by the union of two former British territories, Tanganyika and Zanzibar. The island of Zanzibar was a British protectorate from 1890 until its independence in 1963; only a month after it had achieved independence, the ruling government was overthrown in a left-wing coup. The president of Tanganyika proposed joining the two states in a federation. Zanzibar's quasi-autonomy within Tanzania eroded by 1977. Secessionist agitation, which began in 1984, continues today.

ZAIRE

representative

• Zaire remains under military rule by President Mobuto Sese Seko, who has held power since 1965. A series of political changes announced in 1990 in the face of broad opposition to the government did little to bring a multiparty system. Security forces responded to anti-government demonstrations with force in mid-1991, killing more than 40 protesters. As a concession to opposition groups, Mobutu proposed appointing a prime minister to share power, only to dismiss the opposition leader offered the position just days after he took office in October 1991. Several Western governments suspended aid to Zaire in late 1991. The national conference that the government had convened to work out a new constitution was suspended in January 1992 and resumed in April 1992.

ASIA

BANGLADESH

sub-state

• Following the 1971 civil war that led to the independence of Bangladesh, 250,000 Pakistani refugees, called Biharis for their original home province, remained in Bangladeshi camps. Most have refused Bangladesh's offer of citizenship in exchange for renouncing their Pakistani passports. The Pakistani government has refused to acknowledge their claims to citizenship.

• For more than two decades, the inhabitants of the Chittagong Hill Tracts of southeastern Bangladesh have sought greater autonomy from the central government. Formed in 1971, the Chittagong Hill Tracts People's Coordination Association and its military wing, the Shanti Bahini, are mainly made up of Buddhist Chakma tribespeople. When the Muslim Bengali government failed to respond to autonomy demands, the Shanti Bahini launched a guerrilla campaign in late 1974 and early 1975. The fighting has led to an estimated 5,000 deaths. At least 30,000 inhabitants fled to India to escape the fighting.

BHUTAN

sub-state

• The Bhutanese monarchy faces growing demands from its Hindu Nepalese minority, concentrated mainly in the south. Although official estimates place the strength of the Nepalese community at 30 percent of the population, some unofficial and foreign sources contend that Nepalese make up 50 percent of the population. The country is dominated politically by the Buddhist Drukpas. Tension between the

Nepalese community and the monarchy has increased since 1988, when the king ordered a census to disenfranchise illegal immigrants and designated 1958 as the cut-off date for legal migration. In 1989, the king promoted the Drukpa conduct, dress, and language for all ethnic groups, and outlawed the teaching of Nepali in schools. In September 1990, throughout southern Bhutan, violent clashes occurred between demonstrating Nepalese and government soldiers. In 1991, a resistance movement gained strength. The demands of the Nepalese range from the freedoms of religion, language, and organization, to transformations in the legal system and political order.

CAMBODIA

representative

• In October 1991, rival Cambodian factions signed U.N.-sponsored peace accords that put an end to a 13-year civil war. The agreement provided for U.N. administration of the country's defense, foreign affairs, finance, and internal security under broad guidance from a twelve-member Supreme National Council, made up of representatives of rebel groups and the former Cambodian government. The United Nations was also charged with helping to organize elections by mid-1993 for a 120-member national assembly, which will draft a constitution, transform itself into a legislature, and form a new Cambodian government.

CHINA

representative

• In June 1989, Chinese troops crushed pro-democracy demonstrations in Tiananmen Square, killing at least 1,000 and wounding thousands more. The demonstrations began in April 1989, when students gathered to mourn the death of former Communist Party Leader Hu Yaobang, who had been ousted from the party after student demonstrations in 1986 and 1987. The demonstrations spread in May 1989 to most of China's major cities. On May 18, five days after students began a hunger strike in Tiananmen Square, an estimated one million people demonstrated in the capital in support of the students. Two days later, the Chinese government imposed martial law.

sub-state

Hong Kong

• Under an 1898 treaty between Britain and China, Hong Kong is to revert to Chinese control in the year 1997. The Sino-British Declaration of 1984 set forth the arrangements for the transfer: Hong Kong would remain a "Special Administrative Region" under Chinese control, with guarantees of independent judicial and political powers. The constitution that will govern Hong Kong, known as the Basic Law, calls for one third of legislative seats to be filled by direct election by 1997, and one half to be filled by direct election by 2003. At the time of the 1984 agreement, polls indicated that 90 percent of Hong Kong residents favored maintaining Hong Kong's colonial status. In the first direct election to Hong Kong's Legislative Council in September 1991, liberal pro-democracy candidates swept the 18 seats at stake with calls for more democratic representation of the people of Hong Kong as 1997 approaches.

Inner Mongolia

• In Inner Mongolia, an autonomous region in northern China, nationalism has reportedly begun to surge. Mongols make up 16 percent of the region's population of 21 million. There are periodic reports of anti-government demonstrations in Inner Mongolia; those reports are sketchy, however, because China does not permit foreign journalists to visit the region.

Taiwan

• The main Taiwanese opposition party, the Democratic Progressive Party, seeks independent sovereignty for Taiwan. The government of Taiwan remains committed to a unified China, and identifies itself as the legitimate government. In December 1991 elections for a National Assembly to revise the constitution, the ruling Kuomintang—or Nationalist Party—won 71 percent of the vote. Independence advocates denied that the vote was a setback, citing election fraud, government control of the news media, and government prohibitions on references to independence in campaign statements.

Tibet

• Tibet enjoyed de facto independence from China between 1911 and 1950, when communist forces invaded the region. A year later, Chinese authorities forced an agreement for Chinese rule upon Tibetan leaders. Tibetans rebelled in 1959 when several provisions of the agreement, including those guaranteeing religious freedom and exempting Tibet from communist-style economic reforms, were violated. The revolt was brutally crushed by the Chinese government. As many as 1.2 million Tibetans died in the uprising and its aftermath. Since 1987, sporadic protests for independence have been violently suppressed. In

1988, the Dalai Lama, Tibet's spiritual leader, scaled down a demand for complete independence and instead proposed greater autonomy for the region. The status of Tibet is complicated by the fact that certain areas historically part of Tibet are not now part of what China recognizes as the Tibet Autonomous Region. For example, government-sponsored immigration of Han Chinese into the Qinqhai province has reduced the Tibetan population to 20 percent in an area where it once formed the majority.

Xinjiang

• Aside from the continuing problems in Tibet, the most serious unrest in China has occurred in the western region of Xinjiang. Xinjiang, with a population of 15 million, is home to most of China's Muslims. In April 1990, Chinese authorities cracked down on an armed rebellion in the region, killing about 50 people. In March 1992, government leaders announced a new crackdown on secessionist activities in the region.

FIJI

indigenous

• Indigenous Fijians make up 46 percent of Fiji's population, while ethnic Indians make up 49 percent. The government has traditionally been controlled by ethnic Fijians. Major ethnic violence broke out following the 1987 election of an Indian-dominated government. The predominantly ethnic Fijian army overthrew the elected government, returning the country to civilian rule in January 1990. An interim government created a constitution that secured the political dominance of ethnic Fijians.

INDIA

sub-state

Assam

• The main guerrilla group in Assam, the United Liberation Front of Assam, began functioning in the mid-1980s and has sought Assam's complete independence from India. Facing an Indian army crackdown, the group declared a cease-fire in December 1991 and seemed likely to accept a constitutional settlement with the central government. The agreement has since been abandoned, and fighting resumed in April 1992.

Manipur

• The United Liberation Front of Manipur (ULF), the main guerrilla group in the northeastern Indian state of Manipur, began its insurrection in the 1960s. Manipur remained a centrally ruled territory until 1972, when it was recognized as a full Indian state. The insurgency continues and the ULF has joined forces with other guerrilla groups in northeastern India.

Nagaland

• The National Socialist Council of Nagaland, the oldest and largest guerrilla group fighting for independence in northeastern India, continues a Naga revolt that began in the 1950s. Nagaland became a separate state in the mid-1980s, but guerrillas still operate against Indian security forces in Nagaland and bordering states.

Punjab

• Members of the Sikh religious sect make up 60 percent of the population of Punjab. Sikh separatists calling for an independent homeland of Khalistan have waged a guerrilla war since 1982. In the five years of central Indian rule over Punjab, which began in 1987, some 12,000 people have died in the conflict.

trans-state

Jammu and Kashmir

• The territory of what was once the autonomous princely state of Kashmir has been disputed between Pakistan and India since 1947 and has twice led to war between the two countries. Under terms for the partition of the Indian subcontinent, the princely states could opt for accession to Muslim Pakistan or to Hindu India, or independence. Kashmir's Hindu monarch chose independence for the predominantly Muslim state. That independence was never realized because a Pakistani-supported uprising in western Kashmir forced Kashmir's leader to ask for Indian intervention in exchange for accession. Under the terms of a U.N.-mediated cease-fire to the conflict between India and Pakistan, Kashmir was divided between the two countries. A U.N. resolution called for a plebiscite in which Kashmiris would choose union with Pakistan or India, but no plebiscite was ever held. India formally made Kashmir part of its territory in 1957. Since the 1962 war between India and China, a portion of Kashmir has been under Chinese control. Kashmir remains a source of tension between India and Pakistan. Two hundred thousand Indian security forces patrol the border between the two countries. The latest wave of violence in Kashmir began in January 1990, resulting in nearly 3,000 deaths. Dozens of guerrilla factions operate in the Vale of Kashmir, where most of the fighting has been concentrated. The guerrilla group that enjoys the most popular support is the Jammu and Kashmir Liberation Front, which calls for an independent Kashmiri state comprising the Indian state of Jammu and Kashmir as well as the territories controlled by Pakistan and China. Pakistan opposes the creation of a separate Kashmiri state and, therefore, has at times trained and armed guerrilla groups that favor accession to Pakistan.

INDONESIA

sub-state

Aceh

• In Aceh, a northern province of Sumatra with a population of 3.4 million, rebels have been fighting for independence from Indonesia. According to human rights groups, since March 1990 Indonesian troops deployed to fight the rebels have killed thousands of civilians.

East Timor

• After ruling East Timor for 400 years, Portugal evacuated its final forces in August 1975. A civil war among pro-Portuguese, pro-independence, and pro-Indonesian forces ensued. The left-wing Revolutionary Front for an Independent East Timor (Fretilin), heavily armed with weapons left behind by Portugal, defeated its rivals and declared East Timor's independence on November 29, 1975. Six days later, Indonesian forces invaded and occupied the territory. A December 22, 1975, resolution of the U.N. General Assembly called upon the government of Indonesia to withdraw from the territory; it has never been enforced. In 1976, when a puppet local parliament voted for integration of East Timor with Indonesia, Indonesia annexed East Timor as its twenty-seventh province. Estimates of how many East Timorese died between 1975 and 1989 as Indonesia strove to crush resistance to its rule vary from 100,000 to 200,000 of an indigenous population of 600,000. Periodic clashes between pro-independence and government forces continue; in November 1991, Indonesian forces fired upon pro-independence demonstrators in the capital city of Dili, killing between 50 and 200.

Irian Jaya

• When Indonesia gained independence in 1949, the Dutch government retained control of Netherlands New Guinea, the western half of the island of New Guinea. The Netherlands surrendered control of the territory to the United Nations in 1963. Indonesia was to administer the territory until a referendum on independence was held before the end of 1969. Indonesia instead annexed the territory as Irian Jaya by convening eight puppet regional assemblies, each of which voted for annexation to Indonesia. The Free Papua Movement (OPM) seeks an independent "West Papua" state.

MYANMAR (formerly BURMA)

representative

- In late 1987 and 1988, a series of nonviolent demonstrations against 25 years of military government brought the resignation of the ruling general Ne Win. After the army suppressed the demonstrations in August and September 1988—causing some 3,000 deaths—a military junta seized power, suspended political rights, and set up the State Law and Order Restoration Council (SLORC) to rule. In May 1990 elections permitted by the SLORC, the pro-democracy opposition party National League for Democracy (NLD) won 392 of 485 parliamentary seats contested. The NLD was not permitted to take power. In December 1990, some NLD leaders formed a shadow government in a region of Myanmar controlled by ethnic Karen rebels. According to human rights groups, some 2,000 dissidents were jailed in the two years after the elections.

sub-state

- Ethnic minorities make up one third of Myanmar's population. Among the groups that have been fighting the central government for independence or autonomy in the last three decades are the Karen, Kachin, Mon, Karenni, and Shan rebels. The army of the Karen, Myanmar's largest ethnic minority, is the oldest and strongest of the rebel groups. The Karen rebels faced fierce challenges in their eastern stronghold from government air strikes and troops in early 1992. Meanwhile, the government stepped up a campaign against the Muslim Rohingyas of the Arakan state in western Myanmar. In early 1992, more than 200,000 Rohingyas poured into Bangladesh to escape repression.

PAPUA NEW GUINEA

sub-state

Bougainville

- Rebels on the island of Bougainville declared it an independent republic in May 1990. The secessionist dispute had its roots in grievances over an Australian-owned copper and gold mine located on the island, for which Bougainville demanded environmental damages and a share of profits. Sabotage attacks forced the mine's closure in May 1989. The Bougainville rebels proceeded to call for complete secession and fought government forces between January and March 1990 until a cease-fire was negotiated. The government responded to the May 1990 independence declaration with a blockade. The fighting and the effects of the blockade caused an estimated 3,000 deaths. In 1991, the Papua New Guinea government reasserted control over much of the island.

PHILIPPINES

sub-state

Mindanao

• Separatist groups on the island of Mindanao have sought an independent Muslim state since 1974. By 1986, 50,000 people had been killed in the conflict. In a November 1989 referendum, a central government autonomy plan was passed by four of 13 southern provinces voting on it. The four provinces were designated the Autonomous Region of Muslim Mindanao, and were granted limited autonomy powers (including local control over social services, public works, tourism, and natural resources). The largest of the guerrilla groups, the Moro National Liberation Front, opposed the arrangement, charging that it granted too little autonomy.

SRI LANKA

sub-state

• The Hindu Tamils of Sri Lanka, concentrated in the north and east of the island, make up 17 percent of the Sri Lankan population. Tensions between the Tamils and the majority Buddhist Sinhalese escalated into a full-scale conflict between Tamil separatists and the Sinhalese government in 1983. The conflict, which has had a number of phases and a variety of combatants, including the Indian army, has resulted in some 20,000 deaths. The ruthless Liberation Tigers of Tamil Eelam (LTTE), the main remaining Tamil guerrilla group, has sought to establish a separate state called Eelam. The LTTE serves as a de facto government in stretches of land it controls in the north.

THAILAND

representative

- The military has dominated politics since 1932, when military leaders launched a coup to transform the absolute monarchy into a constitutional monarchy. In 1991, the first elected civilian government in fifteen years was overthrown in the country's seventeenth coup attempt. In April 1992, the coup's leader, General Suchinda Kraprayoon, was appointed prime minister. Beginning on May 4, as many as 100,000 pro-democracy demonstrators gathered to call for Suchinda's resignation because he had never faced direct election. Between May 17 and May 20, the army cracked down on the protesters, killing at least 48 and perhaps 100 people and imprisoning more than 3,000. Suchinda resigned on May 24; shortly thereafter, the parliament passed a constitutional amendment requiring that future prime ministers be elected, not appointed. The interim prime minister called for general elections to be held on September 13, 1992.

EUROPE

BELGIUM

sub-state

- Belgium is in the process of revising its constitution, with the aim of federalizing the state. Disputes between the Flemish-speaking north (Flanders) and the French-speaking south (Wallonia) have brought numerous constitutional crises. In November 1991 elections, nationalist and extremist parties calling for further devolution of power to the regions received increased support.

BULGARIA

sub-state

- Nearly one quarter of Bulgaria's population is made up of minorities. In the late 1980s, the communist Bulgarian government began a campaign of cultural assimilation against the country's one million ethnic Turks, leading to the exodus of 350,000. The policy's reversal in January 1990 brought protests among ethnic Bulgarians. In October 1991 parliamentary elections, the Movement for Rights and Freedom (MRF), which represents ethnic Turks, won 24 seats. The country's new major political party, the Union of Democratic Forces, failed to win a majority, leaving the MRF with a key role in the new government and delaying the government's formation.

CYPRUS

sub-state/trans-state/representative

• Inter-communal fighting broke out in Cyprus in late 1963, three years after the island gained its independence from Britain. Cyprus has been divided since 1974, when Turkey invaded following an attempted coup by right-wing Cypriots against the constitutional leader, Archbishop Makarios. Some of the coup-plotters favored unity with Greece. Some 150,000 Greek Cypriots were displaced from the north during the Turkish invasion. Turkish Cypriots proclaimed the Turkish Republic of Northern Cyprus in the occupied northern third of the island, where Turkey now stations some 35,000 soldiers. Only Turkey has recognized the republic, which the United Nations has declared illegal. Twenty-one hundred U.N. forces are deployed along the "green line" separating the northern and southern portions of the island. In mid-1992, U.N.-sponsored talks commenced to create a "bizonal and bicommunal federal state" in which the territory of the Turkish Cypriot zone would be reduced and a new Cypriot legislature would be established with a lower chamber having a 70–30 Greek-Turkish ratio and an upper chamber with a 50–50 ratio.

CZECHOSLOVAKIA

sub-state

Slovakia

• Slovakia briefly existed as an independent state under Hitler's control during World War II. In 1991 and 1992, a coalition of forces pressed for the republic's independence. Former Czechoslovak President Vaclav Havel's proposal for a referendum in all of Czechoslovakia on the question of independence for Slovakia was rejected by Slovak leaders, because the population of the Czech republic is twice that of the Slovak republic. In March 1992, a month after the Slovak parliament rejected a draft treaty aimed at solving the dispute, a congress of Slovak groups called for the creation of a pluralistic, democratic, and neutral Slovak state. A number of parties adopted a declaration of sovereignty as part of their platforms for June 1992 parliamentary elections. In Slovakia, the nationalist Movement for a Democratic Slovakia, led by the staunchly pro-independence Vladimir Meciar, won 35 percent of the vote. In the Czech republic, in contrast, 30 percent of the voters supported the right-wing Civic Democratic Party. The result was a polarized federal parliament. The Czech and Slovak leaders agreed to form a smaller federal government and set up a process by which the Czech and Slovak parliaments will agree by September 30, 1992, whether or how to break up the state. Hungarian leaders in Slovakia, meanwhile, have declared that they will seek more autonomy within an independent Slovakia.

ESTONIA

• One of the three Baltic republics incorporated into the Soviet Union in 1940, Estonia declared itself to be in a "transitional" phase toward independence on March 30, 1990. In a March 3, 1991, referendum, 78 percent of Estonians voted for independence. The parliament declared Estonia's full independence following the failed August coup in Moscow; that declaration was soon recognized by the international community. The United States announced on September 2, 1991, that it would establish full diplomatic relations with Estonia, and the post-coup Soviet State Council recognized Estonia's independence on September 6.

FRANCE

trans-state

Basque regions

• The main French Basque organization, Those of the North, is closely linked to Spain's terrorist Basque Homeland and Liberty (ETA). The Basque language and culture is distinct from that of France or Spain; the ETA seeks the establishment of an independent Basque state comprising Basque-populated areas in both France and Spain.

sub-state

Brittany

• Both moderate and radical regional groups operate in Brittany, a region in France with a distinct language and culture. These groups include the Breton Democratic Union, which seeks autonomy by nonviolent means, as well as the separatist Liberation Front of Brittany–Breton Republican Army.

Corsica

• The island of Corsica has seen 15 years of nationalist violence. The main clandestine nationalist movement, Front de Liberation Nationale de La Corse, calls for complete independence from France. Polls indicate that 44 percent of the population would like greater autonomy, while only six percent favors complete independence.

anti-colonial

New Caledonia

• New Caledonia's native Melanesians (Kanaks) pressed for independence in the early 1980s. French president François Mitterrand proposed a plan involving five years of autonomy for the region, to culminate in a referendum on independence in 1989. The plan was rejected in a November 1984 referendum. Three years later, in a second referendum largely boycotted by Kanaks, the electorate voted in favor of remaining part of France. In 1989, France and New Caledonia reached agreement on a new timetable, with a referendum on independence to be held in 1998.

LATVIA

• One of three Baltic republics incorporated into the Soviet Union in 1940, Latvia declared itself to be in a "transitional" phase toward independence on May 4, 1990. In a March 3, 1991, referendum, 74 percent of Latvian voters endorsed independence. Latvia declared full independence following the failed August 1991 coup in Moscow and was soon recognized by the international community. The United States announced on September 2, 1991, that it would establish full diplomatic relations with Latvia, and the post-coup Soviet State Council recognized Latvia's independence on September 6.

LITHUANIA

• Lithuania, one of three Baltic republics incorporated into the Soviet Union in 1940, declared independence on March 11, 1990. Soviet President Mikhail Gorbachev declared the step illegal and established an economic blockade. Following a January 1991 crackdown in Lithuania by Soviet troops, 90 percent of Lithuanians voted in a nonbinding plebiscite for secession from the Soviet Union. After the failed August 1991 coup in Moscow, the Baltics were recognized by the international community. The United States announced on September 2, 1991, that it would establish full diplomatic relations with Lithuania, and the post-coup Soviet State Council recognized Lithuania's independence on September 6.

ROMANIA

sub-state

Transylvania

• Romania's two million ethnic Hungarians live mainly in the old Hungarian province of Transylvania. The majority advocate more autonomy within Romania rather than an independent state. The Hungarian Democratic Union of Romania is the second largest party in parliament. In March 1992, ethnic Hungarians launched protests against the Romanian government, seeking the right to educate their children in their own language.

SPAIN

trans-state

Basque Provinces

• One of 17 autonomous regions, the Basque Provinces' culture and language is distinct from that of the rest of Spain. Several moderate nationalist groups, including the ruling party, support autonomy and reject violent separation. Sporadic terrorist acts involving the separatist Basque Homeland and Liberty (ETA) group have resulted in at least 600 deaths in the past 15 years. The ETA seeks the establishment of an independent Basque state comprising Basque-populated areas in both Spain and France.

sub-state

Catalonia

• Two main separatist groups operate in the autonomous region of Catalonia: Free Land and the Movement for the Defense of the Land. Pro-independence parties typically receive less than 10 percent of the vote.

UNITED KINGDOM

sub-state

Northern Ireland

• Catholics in the six northern Irish counties, collectively known as Ulster, have called for union with the Republic of Ireland. At the insistence of Protestant inhabitants, the six counties remained part of the United Kingdom in 1921 when Ireland's other 21 counties gained home rule and eventually independence. In 1968 and 1969, Catholic complaints of discrimination by the dominant Protestant population escalated into the violent disturbances that continue today, resulting in 3,000 deaths between 1969 and 1992. Legislative and executive powers were transferred to Britain in 1972, and Britain has maintained direct rule since. In mid-1992, the British government announced a new round of talks involving the broadest political spectrum of any talks on

Northern Ireland's status to date: the British and Irish governments, together with both Catholic and Protestant leaders in Northern Ireland.

Scotland

• Within the United Kingdom, Scotland has its own legal and educational system and local government, but no parliament. Eighty percent of Scots favor the creation of a Scottish parliament. The Scottish National Party, which holds three seats in the British parliament, advocates an independent Scotland within the European Community.

Wales

• The Welsh Nationalist Party (WNP) seeks greater autonomy for Wales within the United Kingdom. The party holds three seats in the British parliament. In 1987, the WNP entered into an alliance with the Scottish National Party for constitutional, economic, and social reform in both regions.

LATIN AMERICA AND THE CARIBBEAN

BRAZIL

indigenous

• Of an Indian population of roughly 2.5 million in Brazil at the time of European conquest, only 100,000 remained in the nineteenth century. Currently the Indian population of 250,000 scattered throughout Brazil makes up less than one percent of the country's total population. Brazil's June 1988 constitution made some positive references to indigenous rights, acknowledging rights to social organization, customs, language, religion, and tradition. At the same time, however, proposals for including a reference to Brazil as a "multiethnic state" in the constitution were rejected.

GUATEMALA

indigenous

Maya Indians

• Indians make up half of Guatemala's population of seven million. Between 1979 and 1984, the Guatemalan government conducted a campaign of terror against Indians, believing them to be supporting or participating in guerrilla activities. The army destroyed 400 Indian villages, killing as many as 80,000 and forcing at least 70,000 to flee to Mexico.

HAITI

representative

- The September 30, 1991, overthrow of Haitian president Jean-Bertrand Aristide brought calls among his supporters for armed "popular resistance" or international military intervention. The Organization of American States (OAS), backed by the United Nations, imposed an embargo and other economic sanctions. Human rights groups estimate that 1,500 Haitians were killed in the months following the coup. The coup and the ensuing economic chaos had led by August 1992 to the exodus of some 37,000 Haitians, of whom 26,000 were returned to Haiti by the U.S. Coast Guard. In May 1992, the United States adopted a policy of automatically returning refugees without processing their claims at the U.S. naval facility at Guantánamo Bay, Cuba. Meanwhile, the OAS has attempted unsuccessfully to negotiate with Haiti's military for Aristide's return to power.

NICARAGUA

indigenous

Miskito

- The Miskito form the main indigenous community on Nicaragua's Atlantic coast. Under British rule during the eighteenth century, they were permitted to maintain an autonomous "Miskito Kingdom." When Nicaragua became independent in 1894, however, the Miskito king was deposed. In the early 1980s, Miskitos were forcibly relocated by the Sandinista government, with some 20,000 fleeing to Honduras. Negotiations between Miskito leaders (representing smaller indigenous communities as well) between 1984 and 1987 culminated in an "Autonomy Statute," which guaranteed certain rights of cultural autonomy.

MIDDLE EAST

IRAN

trans-state

Kurds

- Kurds make up 10 percent of the total Iranian population. Led by the Kurdish Democratic Party of Iran (KDPI), they have sought to establish an autonomous Kurdistan since 1945.

IRAQ

trans-state/sub-state/representative

Kurds

• Some 3.5 of 25 million Kurds live in Iraq. Following the Gulf war, a Kurdish uprising was suppressed by Iraqi troops. Approximately one million Kurds fled to Iran and half later returned; 400,000 fled to Turkey and later returned. The allied coalition forces established and maintain a buffer zone in Iraq. Eight Kurdish parties in northern Iraq make up the Kurdish Front; the two main groups are the Kurdish Democratic Party (led by Massoud Barzani) and the Patriotic Union of Kurdistan (led by Jalal Talabani). Unlike the Turkish Kurds, the Iraqi Kurds have shown a willingness to accept autonomy rather than complete independence, although negotiations with the Iraqi government have broken down. In May 1992, the Kurds of northern Iraq held their first-ever free elections, with 88 percent of the electorate voting for a regional parliament. See discussion on pages 38–44.

sub-state/representative

Shia

• Shiite Muslims make up 55 percent of Iraq's population and have periodically rebelled against the Iraqi government, which is dominated by Sunni Muslims. The Shia have been brutally repressed under the government of Saddam Hussein; in 1991, they raised an unsuccessful rebellion in southern Iraq. The rebellion was led by three main Iraqi Shiite opposition movements—the Supreme Council of Islamic Revolution in Iraq, the Islamic Call, and the Organization for Islamic Action. See discussion on pages 40–44.

PALESTINIAN MOVEMENT

• The Palestine National Council declared an independent state of Palestine in 1988. The Council cited a 1947 U.N. General Assembly resolution partitioning Palestine into a Jewish and Arab state as providing a legal basis for a right to national sovereignty and self-determination. By mid-1989, 90 countries, including all Arab states except Syria, had recognized either the state or the declaration. A four-year Palestinian uprising in the West Bank and Gaza continues. Talks between Israeli and Palestinian representatives commenced in late 1991, continued through mid-1992, and may lead to political and territorial autonomy or other forms of self-government for Palestinians in the West Bank and Gaza.

TURKEY

trans-state/sub-state

Kurds

• Twelve million of 25 million Kurds live in Turkey. Until early 1991, Turkey denied the existence of the Kurds as a minority; it was forbidden to speak Kurdish in public, listen to Kurdish music, or publish in Kurdish. The Marxist Kurdish Worker's Party (PKK) has been fighting to form a separate Kurdish state since 1984, and has at times been armed by Iraq.

NORTH AMERICA

CANADA

sub-state

Quebec

• Quebec, with a 78 percent French-speaking majority, has called for a radically decentralized confederation. After two English-speaking provinces rejected the 1990 Meech Lake accord, which would have redefined Quebec's ties to Canada, polls indicated 70 percent support among Quebecers for a break with Canada. Unless a new agreement is reached, Quebec will hold a plebiscite by October 26, 1992, on whether to remain part of Canada. Mid-1992 proposals for a revision of Canada's constitution would have accorded Quebec status as a "distinct society" with special laws, culture, and traditions that deserve special protection.

indigenous

Cree Indians

• Independence for Quebec is resisted by the Cree Indians, who occupy much of the northern lands of Quebec and who wish to remain in federation with Canada.

Inuit

• In May 1992, 54 percent of voters in the Northwest Territories backed a proposed boundary for the region's partition and the creation of a territory to be known as Nunavut. The new region will be populated mainly by Inuit. The creation of Nunavut is part of a broader agreement signed in December 1991, whereby the Inuit will get title to 20 percent of the land in the new territory and a $1.4 billion settlement to be paid over 14 years. The agreement must be ratified by Northwest Territories voters in November 1992. Another indigenous group, the Dene Indians, opposes the partition of the Northwest Territories, arguing that the proposed boundary cuts across its traditional lands. The Dene are negotiating with the Canadian government for the establishment of their own territory.

UNITED STATES

anti-colonial

Puerto Rico

• Puerto Rico gained the status of a commonwealth in free association with the United States in 1952. In a 1967 referendum, 60 percent of voters supported maintaining that arrangement, while 39 percent called for full statehood for Puerto Rico and less than one percent called for independence. In 1989, the U.S. Senate and House of Representatives began working on bills for a new vote on Puerto Rico's status, but failed to resolve differences between them. In a December 1991 plebiscite, 53 percent of Puerto Rican voters called for commonwealth status, 45 percent for statehood, and 10 percent for independence.

indigenous

Native Americans

• As many as 14 million Native Americans inhabited what is now the United States before European settlers arrived. By the twentieth century, only 250,000 remained. The U.S. government remains largely indifferent to the 300 tribes living in the United States today; while the United States acknowledges a unique political status for Native Americans, federal legislation has consistently eroded their sovereignty. The government faces a number of court challenges in which Native Americans charge violation of treaty provisions regarding land and resource control.

SUCCESSOR STATES TO THE SOVIET UNION

ARMENIA

• On August 23, 1990, Armenia's parliament adopted a declaration of sovereignty that called for the supremacy of the Armenian constitution over that of the Soviet Union, the creation of a national currency, and the creation of armed forces. The republic boycotted the March 17, 1991, referendum on the preservation of the Soviet Union. Ninety-four percent of the electorate voted and 99 percent of those voting advocated secession in a September 21, 1991, independence referendum (scheduled months before the August coup in Moscow). Two days later, the parliament issued a declaration of full independence. Armenia was one of eight republics to sign an economic accord designed to create a "common economic space" on issues including trade, currency, banking, and customs procedures in October 1991. But Armenia refused to participate in negotiations for a new union treaty in November. With the collapse of the Soviet Union, Armenia joined the Commonwealth of Independent States. Armenia was recognized and offered full diplomatic ties by the United States on December 25, 1991.

AZERBAIJAN

• Azerbaijan boycotted the March 17, 1991, referendum on the preservation of the Soviet Union. In the aftermath of the attempted coup in Moscow, the parliament issued a declaration of independence on August 30, 1991. The republic refused to sign the October 1991 economic accord or participate in negotiations for a new union treaty in November. Azerbaijan joined the Commonwealth of Independent States in December 1991 as the Soviet Union unraveled. The statehood of the former republic was recognized by the United States on December 25, 1991; diplomatic ties were extended in mid-February 1992. In the wake of military setbacks in its conflict with Armenia over Nagorno-Karabakh, Azerbaijani president Ayaz Mutalibov was forced to resign from his post in March 1992. In June 1992 presidential elections, nationalist leader Abulfez Elchibey emerged as the victor, raising fears that fighting in Nagorno-Karabakh would intensify.

trans-state

Nagorno-Karabakh

• An enclave in Muslim Azerbaijan populated largely by Christian Armenians, Nagorno-Karabakh has been disputed between Armenia and Azerbaijan for more than four years. Nagorno-Karabakh has been administered by Azerbaijan since 1923. Fighting broke out in February 1988 after the region's legislature voted to break from Azerbaijan and join Armenia. Azerbaijan responded with a blockade of food and other supplies. Soviet troops were dispatched to the region in May 1989. Although Russian president Boris Yeltsin brokered a cease-fire between the two republics in September 1991, fighting continued and intensified; Azerbaijan annulled the region's autonomous status in November 1991. Ninety-nine percent of voters supported a December 10, 1991, referendum on independence from Azerbaijan, although

Nagorno-Karabakh's Azerbaijani population boycotted the vote. Nagorno-Karabakh requested but was not granted membership in the Commonwealth of Independent States. Several attempts at mediation in late 1991 and early 1992 by Iran, Turkey, the Conference on Security and Cooperation in Europe, and the United Nations failed. By mid-1992, more than 2,000 people had died in the conflict.

Kurds

• The Kurdish population in Azerbaijan, located between the western border of Nagorno-Karabakh and the Armenian-Azerbaijani frontier, has reportedly taken up arms to demand the restoration of an autonomous region that existed between 1923 and 1929. Kurds occupy the strategic town of Lachin and nearby areas; in May 1992, Kurdish insurgents were involved in the fighting that ultimately dislodged Azerbaijani forces from Lachin.

BELARUS

• On July 27, 1990, the parliament of Belarus declared its laws to be sovereign over those of the central government. Following the failed August 1991 coup in Moscow, the parliament issued a declaration of independence. Along with Russia and Ukraine, Belarus formed the Commonwealth of Independent States on December 8, 1991. The United States recognized Belarus and offered full diplomatic ties on December 25, 1991.

GEORGIA

• On November 19, 1989, the Georgian parliament declared the sovereignty of its laws over those of the central government. The move occurred five days after parliamentary elections in which pro-independence candidates secured overwhelming support. Refusing to participate in Soviet president Mikhail Gorbachev's referendum on a new union in March 1991, Georgia instead held a referendum on independence, which passed with nearly 99 percent of the vote. On April 9, 1991, two years after a Soviet crackdown on demonstrators in the capital city of Tbilisi, the Georgian parliament declared the republic's independence. In December, the United States recognized Georgia's statehood but did not establish diplomatic relations, pending a resolution of Georgia's civil disorder and commitments to responsible security policies and respect for human rights. Following fighting in the Georgian capital of Tbilisi between supporters and opponents of President Zviad Gamsakhurdia, which left scores dead and hundreds wounded, opposition forces took control of the government. Former Soviet foreign minister Eduard Shevardnadze returned to Georgia, promising to lead the transition to civilian government. On March 24, 1992, the United States established diplomatic relations with Georgia in light of its commitment to conduct parliamentary elections and to restore civilian rule. Georgia was the only non-Baltic republic not to join the Commonwealth of Independent States.

sub-state/trans-state

Abkhazia

• Abkhazia's population is 46 percent Georgian and 17 percent Abkhazian, but the autonomous region's government is dominated by Abkhazians. In July 1992, Abkhazia's ruling body annulled the republic's 1978 constitution and declared the constitution of 1925 to be in effect. Under that constitution, Abkhazia had been designated as a sovereign state. Fighting broke out in August 1992 between Georgians and Abkhaz separatists. Some of the separatists argue for union of Abkhazia with territory in the north Caucasus of Russia.

trans-state

South Ossetia

• South Ossetia, an autonomous region within Georgia, proclaimed itself a full republic of the Soviet Union in September 1990. Georgia's decision to abolish South Ossetia as a territorial unit brought unrest in December 1990. By mid-1992, the conflict had escalated, as South Ossetia continued to press for union with the Russian autonomous republic of North Ossetia. Russia and Georgia signed an agreement on June 24 on a cease-fire and the stationing of peacekeeping troops on the border. A force of 1,000 peacekeeping troops from Russia, 200 from Georgia, and a small contingent of South and North Ossetians was created to enforce the cease-fire.

KAZAKHSTAN

• With its large non-Kazakh population, Kazakhstan was careful not to issue a provocative declaration of sovereignty when other republics did so. Instead, on October 25, 1990, the republic's parliament declared the sovereignty of its laws in the areas of natural resources and technology over those of the central government. Kazakhstan and Russia were the only two republics not to have issued a declaration of independence from the Soviet Union by November 1991. Kazakhstan was one of the 11 non-Baltic republics that agreed to form the Commonwealth of Independent States, and one of the six new states offered full diplomatic recognition by the United States on December 25, 1991.

KYRGYZSTAN

• In the aftermath of the failed Moscow coup, Kyrgyzstan's parliament declared full independence on August 31, 1991. One of 11 non-Baltic republics to form the Commonwealth of Independent States after the unraveling of the Soviet Union, Kyrgyzstan was offered full diplomatic recognition by the United States on December 25, 1991.

trans-state

• Twelve percent of Kyrgyzstan's population is Uzbek. In June 1990, 200 people were killed in the southwestern town of Osh in riots between Uzbeks and Kyrgyz. In mid-1992, certain regions of Kyrgyzstan were calling for accession to Uzbekistan.

MOLDOVA

• Moldova declared the sovereignty of its laws over those of the central government on June 23, 1990, and boycotted Mikhail Gorbachev's March 1991 referendum on a new union treaty. Moldova's parliament issued a declaration of full independence on August 27, 1991, days after the failed coup in Moscow. The republic initially rejected but later signed the October 1991 economic accord; Moldova refused to participate in November 1991 discussions on Gorbachev's proposal for a new decentralized union. One of 11 republics to join the Commonwealth of Independent States, Moldova was recognized by the United States on December 25, 1991, although the United States declined to establish full diplomatic ties until February 18, 1992. Part of Romania from 1918 to 1940 and annexed by the Soviets under an agreement with Nazi Germany, Moldova has a mainly ethnic Romanian population. The ethnic Romanian majority seeks economic and cultural integration, and possible reunification, with Romania.

sub-state / trans-state

Dniester region

• The Dniester region in eastern Moldova, whose population of 600,000 is made up mainly of ethnic Russians and Ukrainians, declared itself an independent republic within the Soviet Union on September 2, 1990, in response to Moldova's declaration of its laws' sovereignty over those of the Soviet Union. After Moldova declared its independence from the Soviet Union in the aftermath of the August 1991 Soviet coup, the Dniester region reaffirmed its status as an independent republic within the Soviet Union. The region's people fear that Moldova will eventually unify with Romania. Violence broke out in December 1991, leading to 500 deaths by mid-1992. Moldova opposes the Dniester region's secession because some 200,000 ethnic Romanians live there and the Dniester valley is an important industrial region. The conflict began to involve Russia when Russian president Boris Yeltsin moved to take direct control of the former Soviet 14th Army, stationed in the Dniester region of Moldova, in April 1992. A week later, Russia's Congress of People's Deputies adopted a resolution supporting the secessionists. Secessionist leaders also hired hundreds of Cossack fighters from the Don region of southern Russia to supplement their Russian and Ukrainian forces. Fourteenth Army forces began fighting in support of the separatists in June 1992. In July 1992, a "peacemaking" force consisting of Russian, Moldovan, and Dniester units was deployed in the region.

sub-state

Gagauzia

• After a referendum, the Turkic-speaking region of Gagauzia declared itself a full republic within the Soviet Union independent of Moldova on August 19, 1990. Like the Dniester region, Gagauzia opposes Moldovan reunification with Romania.

RUSSIA

• Russia declared its laws to be sovereign over those of the Soviet Union on June 12, 1990. Following the failed August 1991 coup, Russia, like Kazakhstan, did not declare its independence. Russia signed the October 1991 economic accord with seven other Soviet republics and initially pledged support for Gorbachev's proposed decentralized union in November. When Gorbachev's efforts to finalize the treaty were rebuffed by republican presidents, Russian president Boris Yeltsin called upon former Soviet republics to join a commonwealth of independent states. Russia, Ukraine, and Belarus formed the Commonwealth of Independent States on December 8, 1991; eight other republics joined later. The United States and the European Community conferred full diplomatic recognition upon Russia on December 25, 1991. Russia assumed the Soviet Union's seat at the United Nations. In March 1992, 18 of 20 of Russia's republics signed a treaty on preserving Russia's federal structure. The treaty gave republics the right to "independent participation" in foreign relations and economic affairs, with Moscow to handle matters relating to defense, the budget, and the money supply. The two regions that rejected the treaty were Chechen-Ingushetia and Tatarstan.

sub-state

Chechen-Ingushetia

• Under nationalist general Dzokhar Dudayev, who was elected president in a vote described as illegal by Moscow in which most Ingush did not participate, the predominantly Muslim autonomous republic of Russia Chechen-Ingush declared itself a full independent republic of the Soviet Union on November 2, 1991. Russian president Boris Yeltsin declared martial law in the republic on November 8, but his decree was overridden by the Russian parliament three days later. The Chechen people sought complete independence, while the Ingush advocated an autonomous republic within the Russian Federation.

Kaliningrad

• Following the failed coup in Moscow and the independence of the Baltic republics, leaders in the Kaliningrad oblast began lobbying for that region to become a fourth Baltic state. The region had already declared a free economic zone and exercised significant autonomy.

Siberia

• The Independent Siberia Party seeks Siberia's independence and the abolishment of all organs of Russian power at the local level. In March 1992 meetings of the Siberian Congress, the party called upon the Siberian Congress to adopt a declaration of independence, but the Congress did not do so.

sub-state/dispersed peoples

Tatarstan

• Tatarstan, an autonomous republic within Russia, declared itself a full-fledged republic on August 30, 1991. The region's population is 48 percent Tatar and 43 percent Russian. While the Tatars are the largest minority in the Russian republic, 70 percent of all Tatars live outside Tatarstan, dispersed throughout the Russian Federation. Despite condemnation by Russian president Boris Yeltsin, Tatarstan held a referendum on independence on March 21, 1992, with 61 percent voting in favor. Tatar leaders have stated that the republic's immediate objective would be to sign a bilateral treaty with Russian.

Volga region

• The autonomous Volga republic was abolished and its ethnic German population deported to Kazakhstan and elsewhere in Central Asia in 1941. Leaders have pressed for the restoration of the region's autonomous status. A July 10, 1992, treaty between Russia and Germany provided for the resettlement of two million ethnic Germans in the region.

TAJIKISTAN

• Tajikistan's parliament declared the sovereignty of its laws over those of the Soviet Union on August 24, 1990, and issued a declaration of independence on September 9, 1991. The republic signed the October 1991 economic treaty and participated in November 1991 negotiations on a new union treaty. One of 11 republics to join the Commonwealth of Independent States, Tajikistan was recognized as a state, but not extended full diplomatic ties, by the United States on December 25, 1991. The United States recognized the government of Tajikistan in mid-February 1992.

representative

• In early 1992, 100,000 pro-democracy demonstrators rallied in Tajikistan's capital city of Dushanbe to demand the resignation of President Rakhman Nabiyev. Nabiyev negotiated with opposition forces to create a coalition government with opposition leaders on May 11, 1992, but was forced to resign four months later.

sub-state / trans-state

• Leaders in the Kulyab and Leninabad oblasts refused to recognize Tajikistan's May 1992 coalition government. The former threatened to secede, while the latter threatened to ask Uzbekistan for annexation.

TURKMENISTAN

• On August 23, 1990, Turkmenistan's parliament declared its laws sovereign over those of the Soviet Union. The parliament declared independence on October 27, 1991, one day after a referendum that showed overwhelming support for independence. One of 11 republics to join the Commonwealth of Independent States, Turkmenistan was recognized as a state, but not extended full diplomatic ties, by the United States on December 25, 1991. The United States recognized the government of Turkmenistan in mid-February 1992.

UKRAINE

• Ukraine declared the sovereignty of its laws over those of the Soviet Union on July 15, 1990; in November 1990, it became the first Soviet republic to introduce its own crude currency. Its parliament issued a declaration of independence on August 24, 1991, to be ratified in a December 1, 1991, referendum. Ukraine initially refused to sign the October 1991 economic accord, and did not participate in Gorbachev's negotiations on a new union in November. In the December referendum, full independence was supported by 90 percent of voters, and Ukraine was soon recognized by some European states and Canada. Along with Belarus and Russia, Ukraine formed the Commonwealth of Independent States on December 8, 1991. Ukraine was recognized and offered full diplomatic ties by the United States on December 25, 1991.

trans-state

Crimea

• A region in Ukraine populated largely by ethnic Russians and Tatars, the Crimea was transferred from Russia to Ukraine in 1954. Just over half of the Crimeans who voted in Ukraine's December 1, 1991, referendum supported Ukrainian independence. Since Ukraine achieved independence, however, ethnic Russians have pressed for independence or accession to Russia. As of mid-1992, tensions between Russia and Ukraine over the region's final status persisted. On May 5, 1992, the Crimean parliament issued a declaration of independence, pending a referendum. The Ukrainian parliament annulled the declaration shortly thereafter. On May 21 the Russian parliament rejected the legality of the Crimea's 1954 transfer. The fifteen northern regions of the Crimea have threatened to secede from a Crimea that seeks to join Russia. On June 1, 1992, a compromise between Ukraine and the Crimea was announced, with Crimea renouncing its independence in favor of broad autonomy and a special economic status.

dispersed peoples

Crimean Tatars

• The Crimean Tatars, forcibly expelled from the Crimea in 1944, oppose calls to join Russia and themselves declared sovereignty over the Crimea in June 1991. Some 200,000 Crimean Tatars have returned to the Crimea, but 300,000 remain scattered throughout the Soviet Union. Crimean Tatars do not recognize the current Crimean parliament; their goal is an autonomous Tatar republic.

sub-state / trans-state

Transcarpathia

• A region in Ukraine comprising 20 different ethnic groups, Transcarpathia was part of Hungary until the end of World War I, when it was incorporated into Czechoslovakia. During World War II, a portion of the region was occupied by Hungary and a portion existed as part of an independent Carpatho-Ukrainian republic. The region was returned to Czechoslovak control at the end of World War II, but then was ceded to the Soviet Union. In a December 1991 referendum, 78 percent of voters favored an autonomous "self-governing administrative territory." Some leaders have pressed for Czechoslovakia to annul the 1945 Czech-Soviet treaty that led to the territory's transfer; Czechoslovakia has largely distanced itself from these demands.

UZBEKISTAN

• Uzbekistan's parliament declared the sovereignty of its laws over those of the central government on June 20, 1991. On August 31, 1991, Uzbekistan declared its independence. Uzbekistan was one of eight republics to sign an economic accord in October, and one of seven republics to participate in Gorbachev's November 1991 negotiations on a new union treaty. Uzbekistan joined the Commonwealth of Independent States as the Soviet Union unraveled; it was recognized, but not offered full diplomatic ties, by the United States on December 25, 1991. The government was extended diplomatic ties in mid-February 1992. Upon independence, Uzbekistan faced ethnic tensions: Russians account for 8 percent of the population, make up the majority of the industrial work force, and are largely unrepresented at high levels of government. These tensions have led to a mass exodus of ethnic Russians.

SUCCESSOR STATES TO YUGOSLAVIA

BOSNIA-HERZEGOVINA

• A republic containing an ethnic mix of 31 percent Serbs, 17 percent Croats, and 44 percent Muslims, Bosnia-Herzegovina declared independence on October 15, 1991. In December 1991 the republic applied for European Community recognition. The report of an EC arbitration commission recommended that an independence referendum be held. Citizens of Bosnia-Herzegovina voted on independence on February 29 and March 1, 1992; 63 percent of the population took part, with 99 percent of those voting favoring independence. The republic's Serb population boycotted the referendum. Fighting erupted among ethnic groups. The republic received recognition from the European Community and the United States in early April 1992. Shortly thereafter, it was consumed by widespread violence among Serbs and Muslims and Croats, leading to at least 7,000 and perhaps as many as 50,000 deaths by mid-1992, with Serbian forces seizing two thirds of Bosnia's territory. After Serbian forces refused to end a blockade of the capital city of Sarajevo, the international community responded by opening a corridor for humanitarian aid to civilians.

sub-state

  • Serbs in Bosnia-Herzegovina proclaimed a separate republic on January 9, 1992, and formally declared independence on April 7, 1992. In May 1992, leaders of Serb and Croat factions in Bosnia agreed to divide Bosnia into Serbian and Croatian regions of control, with a small territorial concession to Bosnia's Muslims. In July 1992, with Serbian forces occupying two thirds of Bosnia's territory, Croat nationalist leaders in Bosnia proclaimed an independent "Croatian Community of Herceg-Bosna" on the remaining third of the territory. The government of Croatia appeared to distance itself from the proclamation.

CROATIA

  • On February 21, 1991 the Croatian parliament adopted legislation giving the government veto power over federal laws deemed dangerous to Croatia's sovereignty. In a May 19, 1991, referendum, 94 percent of voters backed independence, although balloting was not held in numerous Serb-dominated Croatian counties. Croatia formally declared independence on June 25, 1991, resulting in a full-scale war with the Serbian-dominated Yugoslav federal army and Serb guerrillas in Croatia. The European Community member states, several other European states, and Canada formally recognized Croatia as an independent state on January 15, 1992. The United States followed with recognition on April 7, 1992. Approximately one third of Croatian territory remained under Serbian control in mid-1992. Deployment of a U.N. peacekeeping force of 14,000 in Croatia began in March 1992.

sub-state/trans-state

Krajina

  • The population of Croatia is 12 percent Serb. On October 1, 1990, Serbs in Croatia declared the republic's predominantly Serb populated counties to be autonomous, after Serb voters had overwhelmingly backed autonomy in an unofficial referendum. On March 17, 1991, Serb leaders in the region declared a separate region of Krajina, with Serb voters calling for unification with Serbia in May.

MACEDONIA

  • In a September 8, 1991, referendum, Macedonians voted overwhelmingly for independence from Yugoslavia; the republic proclaimed its independence from Yugoslavia on November 17, 1991. The republic applied for, but was denied, recognition by the European Community on January 15, 1992, largely because of Greek concerns that the use of the name "Macedonia" by the Yugoslav republic signalled territorial ambitions against northern Greece. Nationalist Serbs have never accepted Macedonians as a separate ethnic group and refer to the republic as "South Serbia."

sub-state

- Macedonia contains an ethnic Albanian minority of 25 percent. Albanians in Macedonia boycotted the September 8, 1991, referendum on independence. In an unofficial referendum a few days later, Albanians voted in favor of autonomy for the largely Albanian eastern part of Macedonia.

SLOVENIA

- A September 27, 1989, amendment to Slovenia's constitution established the republic's right to secede from Yugoslavia. In a December 23, 1990, plebiscite, 88 percent of voters backed independence from Yugoslavia by the end of June 1991. Slovenia issued its declaration of independence on June 25, 1991, and fought Serbian troops to a standstill in the brief conflict that ensued. On January 15, 1992, the European Community, several other European states, and Canada recognized Slovenia as an independent state. The United States recognized Slovenia on April 7, 1992.

MONTENEGRO and SERBIA (formed as FEDERAL REPUBLIC OF YUGOSLAVIA in April 1992)

MONTENEGRO

- The sparsely populated, underdeveloped republic of Montenegro cooperates closely with Serbia. Like Serbia, Montenegro has remained committed to some form of Yugoslav federation and did not apply to the European Community for recognition as an independent state. On February 1, 1992, approximately 10,000 Montenegrins demonstrated in favor of an independent state of Montenegro. Four days later, however, Montenegro and Serbia pledged to form a new federal state, a step approved by 96 percent of voters in a March referendum in Montenegro. Slavic Muslims and Albanians, who make up 25 percent of the population, boycotted the referendum. Montenegro and Serbia officially declared a new Federal Republic of Yugoslavia on April 27, 1992.

SERBIA

sub-state

Kosovo

• A province in southern Serbia with two million people, 90 percent of whom are ethnic Albanians, Kosovo was granted autonomy under the 1974 constitution. After that status was revoked by Serbia in 1989, Albanian members of parliament declared Kosovo a republic independent of Serbia. Serbia followed by dissolving Kosovo's parliament and imposing direct rule on the province. September 1990 amendments to the Serbian constitution formally stripped Kosovo of autonomous status. Kosovo declared independence in October 1991, after an unauthorized referendum in which voters overwhelmingly endorsed independence. In May 1992, Kosovo defied Serbian authorities by holding elections for a president and a regional assembly.

Vojvodina

• The autonomy of Vojvodina, like that of Kosovo, was formally revoked by Serbia in September 1990. Fifty-four percent of the province's two million people are Serbs, 19 percent ethnic Hungarians, and four percent Croats. In April 1992, the Democratic Community of Hungarians in Vojvodina (DCHV) adopted a "charter" on self-determination for the Hungarian community, calling for individual and collective provisions on autonomy in Hungarian regions and equal rights for other ethnic groups in those regions. According to the DCHV, 20,000 Hungarians have been forced by Serbs to flee Vojvodina. By May 1992, other non-Serbs were reportedly being forcibly expelled from Vojvodina as Serb refugees from Bosnia-Herzegovina were being resettled there.

trans-state

Novi Pazar Sanjak

• A region in Serbia and Montenegro formerly belonging to Bosnia-Herzegovina, Novi Pazar Sanjak has a Muslim minority of 250,000 that demanded autonomy and links to Bosnia in late 1990.

APPENDIX SOURCES

Amnesty International:
  Report 1990
  Report 1991
Africa Report
Asian Survey
Beijing Review
Christian Science Monitor
Cyprus Newsletter
East European Reporter
Economist
Far Eastern Economic Review
Foreign Broadcast Information Service *Daily Reports:*
  Central Eurasia
  China
  East Europe
  East Asia
  Latin America
  Near East & South Asia
  Sub-Saharan Africa
  West Europe
Financial Times
Foreign Policy
Freedom House:
  Freedom in the World—1991–1992
  Freedom in the World—1990–1991
International Herald Tribune
Journal of Democracy
Journal of Soviet Nationalities
Keesing's Political Dissent
Keesing's Revolutionary and Dissident Movements
Latin American Perspectives
Los Angeles Times
New Republic
New York Times
Newsweek
Political Handbook of the World: 1991

Radio Free Europe/Radio Liberty:
    RFE/RL *Research Report*
    RFE/RL *Daily Report*
Stockholm International Peace Research Institute:
    SIPRI Yearbook 1991
Third World Quarterly
Time
U.S. News and World Report
U.S. Department of State:
    Country Reports on Human Rights Practices for 1991
Wall Street Journal
Washington Post

STUDY GROUP PARTICIPANTS

CARNEGIE PROJECT ON SELF-DETERMINATION

Morton H. Halperin (Co-Chairman)
Carnegie Endowment for International Peace

David J. Scheffer (Co-Chairman)
Carnegie Endowment for International Peace

Patricia L. Small (Rapporteur)
Carnegie Endowment for International Peace

Pauline Baker
Aspen Institute

James Clad
*Carnegie Endowment for
International Peace*

Gregory Craig
Williams & Connolly

Lloyd N. Cutler
Wilmer, Cutler & Pickering

Michael W. Doyle
*Woodrow Wilson School of
Public and International
Affairs
Princeton University*

Leon Fuerth
*Office of U.S. Senator
Albert Gore*

Paul Goble
*Carnegie Endowment for
International Peace*

Stanley J. Heginbotham
Social Science Research Council

Frank Koszorus, Jr.
*Paul, Hastings, Janofsky &
Walker*

Carol Lancaster
*School of Foreign Service
Georgetown University*

Donald McHenry
*School of Foreign Service
Georgetown University*

Stephen Rickard
*Office of U.S. Senator Daniel
Patrick Moynihan*

Stanley Roth
Subcommittee on Asian and
Pacific Affairs
U.S. House of Representatives

Leon Sigal
The New York Times

Edwin M. Smith
University of Southern
California Law Center

Louis B. Sohn
The National Law Center
The George Washington
University

Jenonne Walker
Woodrow Wilson International
Center for Scholars

Note: Study group members' affiliations are listed as they were on August 1, 1992. The analysis and views in this book are those of the authors and do not necessarily reflect the views of any individual member of the study group or any institution or governmental body with which the member is or has been affiliated.

BIBLIOGRAPHY

Alexander, Yonah and Robert A. Friedlander, eds. *Self-Determination: National, Regional, and Global Dimensions.* Boulder: Westview Press, 1980.

Azar, Edward E. and John W. Burton, eds. *International Conflict Resolution.* Boulder: Lynne Rienner Publishers, 1986.

Beitz, Charles R. *Political Theory and International Relations.* Princeton: Princeton University Press, 1979.

Berg, Jonathan. "The Right to Self-Determination." *Public Affairs Quarterly* 5 (July 1991): pp. 211–25.

Bilder, Richard B. "Can Minorities Treaties Work?" In *The Protection of Minorities and Human Rights,* edited by Yoram Dinstein, 59–82. The Hague: Nijhoff, 1992.

Boutros-Ghali, Boutros. *An Agenda for Peace.* New York: United Nations, 1992.

Bowett, D.W. *The Law of International Institutions.* 4th ed. London: Stevens & Sons, 1982.

Bowett, D.W. *United Nations Forces.* New York: Praeger, 1964.

Brilmayer, Lea. "Secession and Self-Determination: A Territorial Interpretation." *Yale Journal of International Law* 16 (1991): pp. 177–202.

Brown, David. "Ethnic Revival: Perspectives on State and Society." *Third World Quarterly* 11 (October 1989): pp. 1–17.

Brownlie, Ian. "An Essay in the History of the Principle of Self-Determination." In *Grotian Society Papers: Studies in the History of the Law of Nations, 1968,* edited by C.N. Alexandrowicz, 90–99. The Hague: Nijhoff, 1970.

Brownlie, Ian. *Principles of Public International Law.* 4th ed. Oxford: Clarendon Press, 1990.

Buchanan, Allen. *Secession: The Morality of Political Divorce from Fort Sumter to Lithuania and Quebec.* Boulder: Westview Press, 1991.

Buchheit, Lee C. *Secession: The Legitimacy of Self-Determination.* New Haven: Yale University Press, 1978.

Buergenthal, Thomas, ed. *Human Rights, International Law and the Helsinki Accord.* New York: Universe Books, 1977.

Burg, Steven L. "The Soviet Union's Nationalities Question." *Current History* 88 (October 1989): pp. 341–62.

Carnegie Endowment National Commission on America and the New World. *Changing Our Ways.* Washington, D.C.: Carnegie Endowment for International Peace, 1992.

Carter, Stephen K. *Russian Nationalism: Yesterday, Today, Tommorow.* New York: St. Martin's Press, 1990.

Cassese, Antonio. *International Law in a Divided World*. Oxford: Clarendon Press, 1986.

Chaliand, Gerard, ed. *People Without a Country: The Kurds and Kurdistan*. London: Zed Press, 1980.

Chen, Lung-Chu. "Self-Determination and World Public Order." *Notre Dame Law Review* 66 (1991): pp. 1287–1297.

Cobban, Alfred. *The Nation State and National Self-Determination*. New York: Thomas Y. Crowell Co., 1969.

Crawford, James. *The Creation of States of International Law*. Oxford: Clarendon Press, 1979.

Cviic, Christopher. *Remaking the Balkans*. New York: Council on Foreign Relations Press, 1991.

Damrosch, Lori Fisler and David J. Scheffer, eds. *Law and Force in the New International Order*. Boulder: Westview Press, 1991.

de St. Jorré, John. *The Nigerian Civil War*. London: Hodder and Stoughton, 1972.

Dinstein, Yoram. *Models of Autonomy*. New Brunswick, New Jersey: Transaction Books, 1981.

Eide, Asbjørn. "Minority Situations: In Search of Peaceful and Constructive Solutions." *Notre Dame Law Review* 66 (1991): pp. 1311–1346.

Emerson, Rupert. "Self-Determination." *American Journal of International Law* 65 (1971): pp. 459–75.

Franck, Thomas M. "The Emerging Right to Democratic Governance." *American Journal of International Law* 86 (1992): pp. 46–91.

Franck, Thomas M. "Legitimacy in the International System." *American Journal of International Law* 82 (1988): pp. 705–59.

Fuller, Graham E. *The Democracy Trap: Perils of the Post-Cold War World*. New York: Dutton, 1991.

Fuller, Graham E. "Soviet Nationalities and Democratic Reform." *Global Affairs* 6 (Winter 1991): pp. 23–39.

Galloway, L. Thomas. *Recognizing Foreign Governments: The Practice of the United States*. Washington, D.C.: American Enterprise Institute, 1978.

Goble, Paul A. "Coping with the Nagorno-Karabakh Crisis." *Fletcher Forum* 16 (Summer 1992): pp. 19–26.

Goble, Paul A. "Forget the Soviet Union." *Foreign Policy* 86 (Spring 1992): pp. 56–65.

Goldmann, Robert B. and A. Jeyaratnam Wilson. *From Independence to Statehood*. London: Frances Pinter, 1984.

Gros-Espiell, Hector. *The Right to Self-Determination: Implementation of United Nations Resolutions*. New York: United Nations, 1980.

Hannum, Hurst. *Autonomy, Sovereignty, and Self-Determination: The Accommodation of Conflicting Rights*. Philadelphia: University of Pennsylvania Press, 1990.

Hannum, Hurst. "Contemporary Developments in the International Protection of the Rights of Minorities." *Notre Dame Law Review* 66 (1991): pp. 1431–1448.

Hannum, Hurst. "New Developments in Indigenous Rights." *Virginia Journal of International Law* 28 (Spring 1988): pp. 649–78.

Henkin, Louis, ed. *The International Bill of Rights: The Covenant on Civil and Political Rights.* New York: Columbia University Press, 1981.

Henkin, Louis, et al. *Right v. Might.* 2d ed. New York: Council on Foreign Relations, 1991.

Heraclides, Alexis. "Secessionist Minorities and External Involvement." *International Organization* 44 (Summer 1990): pp. 341–78.

Heraclides, Alexis. *The Self-Determination of Minorities in International Politics.* London: Frank Cass, 1991.

Horowitz, Donald L. *Ethnic Groups in Conflict.* Berkeley: University of California Press, 1985.

Hurst, Michael. *Key Treaties of the Great Powers.* Vol. I. *1814–1870.* New York: St. Martin's Press, 1972.

Iglar, Richard F. "The Constitutional Crisis in Yugoslavia and the International Law of Self-Determination: Slovenia's and Croatia's Right to Secede." *Boston College International and Comparative Law Review* 15 (1992): pp. 213–39.

Independent Commission on International Humanitarian Issues. *Indigenous Peoples: A Global Quest for Justice.* London: Zed Books, 1987.

Jacobson, John R. *The Territorial Rights of Nations and Peoples.* Lewiston, New York: Edwin Mellen Press, 1989.

James, Alan. *Sovereign Statehood.* London: Allen and Unwin, 1986.

Johnson, Harold S. *Self-Determination within the Community of Nations.* Leyden: Sijthoff, 1967.

Kelsen, Hans. *The Law of the United Nations.* New York: Frederick A. Praeger, 1950.

Király, Béla K., Peter Pastor, and Ivan Sanders, eds. *Essays on World War I: A Case Study on Trianon.* Highland Lakes, New Jersey: Atlantic Research and Publications, 1982.

Knight, David B. "Territory and People or People and Territory? Thoughts on Post-colonial Self-Determination." *International Political Science Review* 6 (1985): pp. 258–72.

Laitin, David D. "The National Uprisings in the Soviet Union." *World Politics* 44 (October 1991): pp. 139–77.

Lansing, Robert. *The Peace Negotiations: A Personal Narrative.* Boston: Houghton Mifflin Co., 1921.

Levitin, Michael J. "The Law of Force and the Force of Law: Grenada, the Falklands, and Humanitarian Intervention." *Harvard International Law Journal* 27 (1986): pp. 621–57.

Lewis, I.M., ed. *Nationalism and Self Determination in the Horn of Africa.* London: Ithaca Press, 1983.

Liu, Leo Y. "Self-Determination, Independence and the Process of Democratization in Taiwan." *Asian Profile* 19 (June 1991): pp. 197–205.

Macartney, W.J. Allan, ed. *Self-Determination in the Commonwealth*. Aberdeen: Aberdeen University Press, 1988.

Markakis, John. *National and Class Conflict in the Horn of Africa*. New York: Cambridge University Press, 1987.

Mayall, James. "Non-intervention, Self-determination and the 'New World Order.'" *International Affairs* 67 (July 1991): pp. 421–29.

McColm, Bruce, et al. *Freedom in the World: Political Rights and Civil Liberties*. New York: Freedom House, 1992.

Minority Rights Group. *Minorities and Autonomy in Western Europe*. London: Minority Rights Group, 1991.

Montville, Joseph V. *Conflict and Peacemaking in Multiethnic Societies*. Lexington, Mass.: Lexington Books, 1990.

Nanda, Ved P. "Self-Determination in International Law: The Tragic Tale of Two Cities—Islamabad (West Pakistan) and Dacca (East Pakistan)." *American Journal of International Law* 66 (1972): pp. 321–36.

Nanda, Ved P. "Self-Determination Under International Law: Validity of Claims to Secede." *Case Western Reserve Journal of International Law* 13 (1981): pp. 257–80.

Nixon, Charles R. "Self-Determination: The Nigeria/Biafra Case." *World Politics* 24 (1972): pp. 479–97.

Oakley, Robin. *Eastern Europe, 1740–1985: Feudalism to Communism*. Minneapolis: University of Minnesota Press, 1986.

Ofuatey-Kodjoe, W. *The Principle of Self-Determination in International Law*. New York: Nellen, 1977.

Olcott, Martha Brill. "The Lithuanian Crisis." *Foreign Affairs* 69 (Summer 1990): pp. 30–46.

Olcott, Martha Brill. "The Slide into Disunion." *Current History* 90 (October 1991): pp. 338–44.

Pomerance, Michla. *Self-Determination in Law and Practice*. Boston: Martinus Nijhoff Publishers, 1982.

Pomerance, Michla. "The United States and Self-Determination: Perspectives on the Wilsonian Conception." *American Journal of International Law* 70 (1976): pp. 1–27.

Ra'anan, Uri, Maria Mesner, Keith Armes, and Kate Martin, eds. *State and Nation in Multi-ethnic Societies*. New York: Manchester University Press, 1991.

Ronen, Dov. *The Quest for Self-Determination*. New Haven: Yale University Press, 1979.

Rosenstock, Robert. "The Declaration of International Law concerning Friendly Relations: A Survey." *American Journal of International Law* 65 (1971): pp. 713–35.

Rusinow, Dennison. "Yugoslavia: Balkan Breakup?" *Foreign Policy* 83 (Summer 1991): pp. 143–59.

Ryan, Kevin. "Rights, Intervention, and Self-Determination." *Denver Journal of International Law and Policy* 20 (Fall 1991): pp. 55–71.

Ryan, Stephen. *Ethnic Conflict and International Relations.* Brookfield, Vermont: Dartmouth Publishing Co., 1990.

Saladin, Claudia. "Self-Determination, Minority Rights, and Constitutional Accommodation: The Example of the Czech and Slovak Federal Republic." *Michigan Journal of International Law* 13 (Fall 1991): pp. 172–217.

Saxena, J.N. *Self-Determination: From Biafra to Bangla Desh.* Delhi: University of Delhi, 1978.

Scheffer, David J. "Toward a Modern Doctrine of Humanitarian Intervention." *The University of Toledo Law Review* 23 (1992): pp. 253–93.

Schöpflin, George. "Nationalism and National Minorities in East and Central Europe." *Journal of International Affairs* 45 (Summer 1991): pp. 51–65.

Shiel, Frederick L., ed. *Ethnic Separatism and World Politics.* Lanham, Maryland: University Press of America, 1984.

Sieghart, Paul. *The International Law of Human Rights.* New York: Oxford University Press, 1983.

Smith, Anthony D. *The Ethnic Revival.* New York: Cambridge University Press, 1981.

Sohn, Louis B. *Cases in United Nations Law.* 2d ed. Brooklyn: Foundation Press, 1967.

Sohn, Louis B. "The Concept of Autonomy in International Law and the Practice of the United Nations." *Israel Law Review* 15 (1980): pp. 180–90.

Sohn, Louis B. "Gradations of Intervention in Internal Conflict." *Georgia Journal of International and Comparative Law* 13 (1983): pp. 225–30.

Sohn, Louis B. "Regional and Other International Responses to Internal Conflicts," *Georgia Journal of International and Comparative Law* 13 (1983): pp. 323–26.

Sohn, Louis B. "Rights, under International Law, of Persons Belonging to National, Ethnic, Religious and Linguistic Minorities." In Georg Brunner and Allan Kagedan, eds. *Minorities in the Soviet Union under International Law.* Cologne, 1988: pp. 13–22.

Sohn, Louis B. and Thomas Buergenthal. *International Protection of Human Rights.* Indianapolis: Bobbs-Merrill, 1973.

Steiner, Henry J. "Ideals and Counter-Ideals in the Struggle Over Autonomy Regimes for Minorities." *Notre Dame Law Review* 66 (1991): pp. 1539–1560.

Stremlau, John J. *The International Politics of the Nigerian Civil War (1967–1970).* Princeton: Princeton University Press, 1977.

Stromseth, Jane E. "Self-Determination, Secession, and Humanitarian Intervention by the United Nations." *Proceedings of the 86th Annual Meeting, American Society of International Law* (forthcoming 1992).

Suhrke, Astri and Lela Garner Noble, eds. *Ethnic Conflict in International Relations.* New York: Praeger, 1977.

Sureda, A. Rigo. *The Evolution of the Right of Self-Determination.* Leyden: Sijthoff, 1973.

Thornberry, Patrick. *Minorities and Human Rights Law.* London: Minority Rights Group, 1991.

Thornberry, Patrick. "Self-Determination, Minorities, Human Rights: A Review of International Instruments." *International and Comparative Law Quarterly* 38 (October 1989): pp. 867–89.

Umozurike, Umozurike Oji. *Self-Determination in International Law.* Hamden, Conn.: Archon Books, 1972.

Van Dyke, Vernon. *Human Rights, Ethnicity, and Discrimination.* Westport, Conn.: Greenwood Press, 1985.

Van Dyke, Vernon. "The Individual, the State, and Ethnic Communities in Political Theory." *World Politics* 29 (1977): pp. 343–69.

Van Dyke, Vernon. "Self-Determination and Minority Rights." *International Studies Quarterly* 13 (September 1969): pp. 226–33.

Verzijl, J.H.W. *International Law in Historical Perspective.* Leyden: Sijthoff, 1968.

Wambaugh, Sarah. *Plebiscites Since the World War.* 2 Vols. Washington, D.C.: Carnegie Endowment for International Peace, 1933.

Whitaker, Ben. *Minorities—A Question of Human Rights?* New York: Pergamon Press, 1984.

Wilson, Heather. *International Law and the Use of Force by National Liberation Movements.* Oxford: Clarendon Press, 1988.

Wyatt, Marilyn, ed. *CSCE and the New Blueprint for Europe.* Washington, D.C.: Georgetown University Institute for the Study of Diplomacy, 1991.

INDEX

ABOUT THE AUTHORS

MORTON H. HALPERIN is a political scientist who has published on a number of issues related to American foreign policy and international security. As of November 1992 he will be a Senior Associate at the Carnegie Endowment for International Peace and Edgar A. Baker Professor of International Affairs at The George Washington University. He has served as member of the senior staff of the National Security Council (1969) and as Deputy Assistant Secretary of Defense for International Security Affairs (1967–69). He is author among many other works of *Nuclear Fallacy* (1987) and *Bureaucratic Politics and Foreign Policy* (1974). He has taught at a number of universities, including Harvard, Columbia, and Yale. Mr. Halperin is Co-Chairman of the Carnegie Project on Self-Determination.

DAVID J. SCHEFFER, an international lawyer, is a Senior Associate at the Carnegie Endowment for International Peace and Adjunct Professor of Law at the Georgetown University Law Center. He previously served on the professional staff of the Committee on Foreign Affairs of the U.S. House of Representatives and was an attorney with the international law firm of Coudert Brothers. He is co-editor and contributing author of *Law and Force in the New International Order* (1991), a contributing author of *Right v. Might: International Law and the Use of Force* (2nd ed., 1991), and a frequent contributor to law reviews and the OP-ED pages of major newspapers. Mr. Scheffer is Co-Chairman of the Carnegie Project on Self-Determination.

PATRICIA L. SMALL, a graduate of Harvard and Radcliffe Colleges, was an editorial assistant at *Foreign Policy* magazine and a research assistant for the Carnegie Project on Self-Determination. She is currently a student at Yale Law School.